# Samuel Beckett's
## *Waiting for Godot*

# Continuum Modern Theatre Guides

Continuum modern theatre guides offer concise, accessible and informed introductions to the key plays of modern times. Each book is carefully structured to offer a systematic study of the play in its biographical, historical, social and political context, an in-depth study of the text, an overview of the work's production history including screen adaptations, and practical workshopping exercises. They also include a timeline and suggestions for further reading which highlight key critical approaches.

*Arthur Miller's Death of a Salesman* Peter L. Hays and Kent Nicholson

*August Wilson's Fences* Ladrica Menson-Furr

*Caryl Churchill's Top Girls* Alicia Tycer

*David Mamet's Oleanna* David K. Sauer

*John Osborne's Look Back in Anger* Aleks Sierz

*Patrick Marber's Closer* Graham Saunders

*Sarah Kane's Blasted* Helen Iball

*Tom Stoppard's Arcadia* John Fleming

*Tony Kushner's Angels in America* Ken Nielsen

**Mark Taylor-Batty and Juliette Taylor-Batty**

# Samuel Beckett's
## *Waiting for Godot*

continuum

**Continuum International Publishing Group**
The Tower Building         80 Maiden Lane
11 York Road             Suite 704, New York
London SE1 7NX      NY 10038

www.continuumbooks.com

**British Library Cataloguing-in-Publication Data**
A catalogue record for this book is available from the British Library.

ISBN:    978-0-8264-9593-8 (hardback)
          978-0-8264-9594-5 (paperback)

**Library of Congress Cataloging-in-Publication Data**
A catalog record for this book is available from the Library of Congress.

Typeset by Newgen Imaging Systems Pvt Ltd, Chennai, India
Printed and bound in Great Britain by MPG Books Ltd, Bodmin, Cornwall

# Contents

# Acknowledgements

The authors would like to acknowledge Faber and Faber Ltd. and Grove/Atlantic, Inc for permission to use material from Samuel Beckett's *Waiting for Godot*.

*WAITING FOR GODOT* by Samuel Beckett Copyright © 1954 by Grove Press, Inc.; copyright © renewed 1982 by Samuel Beckett

*WAITING FOR GODOT* by Samuel Beckett © Faber and Faber Ltd – © 1965 by Faber and Faber

All references throughout this book to the text of *Waiting for Godot* are to this edition: Beckett, Samuel (1965), *Waiting for Godot*. London: Faber and Faber.

# General Preface

## *Continuum Modern Theatre Guides*

Volumes in the series Continuum Modern Theatre Guides offer concise and informed introductions to the key plays of modern times. Each book takes a close look at one particular play's dramaturgical qualities and then at its various theatrical manifestations. The books are carefully structured to offer a systematic study of the play in its biographical, historical, social and political context, followed by an in-depth study of the text and a chapter which outlines the work's production history, examining both the original productions of the play and subsequent major stage interpretations. Where relevant, screen adaptations will also be analysed. There then follows a chapter dedicated to workshopping the play, based on suggested group exercises. Also included are a timeline and suggestions for further reading.

Each book covers:

- Background and context
- Analysis of the play
- Production history
- Workshopping exercises

The aim is to provide accessible introductions to modern plays for students in both Theatre/Performance Studies and English, as well as for informed general readers. The series includes up-to-date coverage of a broad range of key plays, with summaries of important critical approaches and the intellectual debates that have illuminated the meaning of the work and made a significant contribution to our broader cultural life. They will enable readers to develop their understanding of playwrights and theatre-makers, as well as inspiring them to broaden their studies.

The Editors:
Steve Barfield, Janelle Reinelt,
Graham Saunders and Aleks Sierz
March 2008

# 1 Background and Context

## Beckett before Godot

*Waiting for Godot* was written in Paris, in French, between 9 October 1948 and 29 January 1949. Its forty-two-year-old author, Samuel Barclay Beckett (1906–89), was an Irish writer who had taken up permanent residence in the French capital over a decade earlier. Beckett rewrote the play in English in 1953, after its first French production, and assisted in the German translation, which he later refashioned for his own Berlin production of the play in 1975. The play was one of the most influential European dramas of the post-war period. When it first made its appearance on the French stage, one critic referred to its impact as 'knocking the dust off the theatre'[1] and another recognized it as 'a profoundly original work' (Lemarchand 1953). Two years later in London it was received as a play that 'jettisons everything by which we recognise theatre' (Tynan 1955) and was later lauded, perhaps with a certain excessive enthusiasm, as 'the laugh hit of two continents' when it opened in Florida, USA, in 1956 (Knowlson 1997, 420). Its rapid success, rising from its impoverished premiere in a small Parisian fringe theatre to international mainstream venues in only a few years, is some indication of how refreshing it was for the theatrical establishment of its time. For its first director, Roger Blin, one of the play's attractions was the confrontational stance that the play adopted in the face of established notions of what made good theatre. He knew the play 'was going to raze to the earth three quarters of the theatre' and this provocation was as attractive to him as its lyrical beauty and thematic appeal (Knapp 1967, 123). This book aims to explain why the play is so important in the history of modern theatre and seeks to examine its key features and the themes it explores.

As a young man, Beckett seemed set on course for a respectable academic career. Having achieved a first-class degree in modern languages (French and Italian) from Trinity College, Dublin in 1927, he worked briefly as a tutor of French and English at Campbell College, Belfast, and then as a *Lecteur d'Anglais* at the École Normale Supérieure in Paris. In 1930, he took up a post as Lecturer in French back in Dublin at Trinity, though he was to resign the position two years later, disillusioned with teaching and determined to pursue his ambition to become a writer. His interest in creative writing, his urge to express his experience of the world, had begun during his years as a scholar, and his first published writings – a short story, 'Assumption' (1929) and a poem *Whoroscope* (1930) – appeared concurrently with his first critical essays 'Dante . . . Bruno. . . Vico. . . Joyce' (1929) and *Proust* (1930). These essays display a keen, youthful erudition and pronounce an allegiance with the principles of an attitude to literature and art that was to be known as modernism: an early twentieth-century break with established literary and artistic traditions in favour of radical forms of experimentation and innovation, as exemplified by the novels of James Joyce.

Beckett had met Joyce in Paris in 1928, and became part of the great Irish author's social circle. He helped him with some research for the work in progress that was to become *Finnegans Wake*, and would, for example, read materials aloud to Joyce, whose eyesight was weak and who appreciated such assistance. Beckett wrote 'Dante. . . Bruno. . . Vico. . . Joyce' at the older writer's suggestion, and in his analysis of Joyce's use of language there are the first suggestions of an artistic credo that he himself would adopt, albeit to far different literary ends. In the essay he wrote of how, in

Joyce, 'form *is* content, content *is* form' (Beckett 1983, 27), in other words the alliance of what is being expressed is dependent upon and interlinked with the manner in which it is expressed. This is something that was later to be symptomatic of his own writing.

Beckett wrote his first extended work of fiction, *Dream of Fair to Middling Women*, between 1931 and 1932, though it was to remain unpublished until after his death. Between 1932 and his eventual decision to establish himself in the French capital in 1937, Beckett circulated between Paris, London and Dublin, with a brief sojourn in Germany. He found attitudes in his native Ireland parochial and small-minded compared to his experiences abroad, and was to be irritated by prudish critical responses to his work there. An interconnected collection of prose stories, which contained reworked extracts from *Dream of Fair to Middling Women*, was published in 1934 under the risqué title *More Pricks Than Kicks*, wittily referencing the Acts of the Apostles (Acts 26: 14). This, and much of the content of the work, met with the disgust of the Irish censors. During this period, he took on pieces of translation work, and pursued his intellectual interests in art, visiting numerous galleries while in Germany. He also wrote his novel *Murphy* which, after forty-two rejections, was eventually published in 1938. The struggle to eke out any sort of living as a writer was neatly captured in something of an in-joke in *Waiting for Godot* when Vladimir tells Estragon that 'You should have been a poet' and Estragon responds by pointing to the ragged state of his clothing and replying 'I was [. . .] Isn't that obvious?' (12).

When war broke out across Europe in September 1939, Beckett was visiting his mother in Ireland. Though possessing a passport from a neutral country, he returned to France the day after it entered the conflict and eventually became involved in the Resistance movement, operating as a compiler and translator of reports of German military movements. His cell was eventually infiltrated in 1942 by the German authorities, and his friends consequently arrested by the Gestapo. He fled with his partner Suzanne Deschevaux-Desmesnil (whom he was to marry in 1961) safely to pass the rest of the war in the secluded village of Roussillon in Vaucluse, forty miles north of Marseilles. Here he worked for a local farmer, named Bonnelly, whose name was to appear in the French text of *Waiting for Godot*, which also located the farmer in Roussillon in the Vaucluse (Beckett 1952, 86). None of the proper nouns were retained in the English text, in which Vladimir can neither remember the name of the man nor the village, and the reference to the Vaucluse was replaced by the 'Macon country'. The reference to the remarkable deep ochre colour of the soil there is, however, kept ('down there everything is red') (62).

In Roussillon, Beckett once again became involved in the Resistance. He assisted in hiding armaments and participated in sorties under the cloak of night to assist in the arms supply chain, sometimes waiting in ditches ready to use force, if necessary, in planned ambushes. Beckett's experiences with the French resistance and his status as exile and refugee are in part captured in *Waiting for Godot*. Resistance liaisons involved rendezvous with unnamed figures whose actual appearances were far from guaranteed, and which might be postponed by ambiguous, anonymous messengers. The purpose or results of interventions were often unknowable and unquantifiable. The risk of violence was commonplace, as was the possibility of having to bear witness to the ill-treatment of others. The experience of 1939–44 was one of waiting for an uncertain future liberation, passing the time in frugal surroundings for days on end with little in the way of intellectual or physical nourishment. All these things form the thematic substance of Beckett's key play. In their escape to Roussillon, Beckett and Suzanne walked long distances by night and slept during daylight in haystacks and ditches. The image of a mutually dependent couple, disoriented and bereft of social context, able to both irritate and console one another, uncertain of their future, alternately clutching at straws of hope and sunk by fear and despair, is clearly central to the expression of *Waiting for Godot*.

## *Waiting for Godot* and Beckett's prose

After the constraints and hardships of the war, Beckett entered a period of extraordinary literary productivity: in the period 1946–50 he completed the novels *Watt*, *Mercier et Camier*, *Molloy*, *Malone meurt* and *L'Innommable* (the latter three forming a trilogy), the plays *Eleuthéria* and *En Attendant Godot*,[2] and a number of shorter stories, texts, poems and pieces of criticism. With the exception of *Watt*, which he had begun much earlier, in 1941, this 'frenzy of writing' (Knowlson 1997, 358) was conducted exclusively in Beckett's adopted language, French. Beckett had already experimented with writing in this language, having composed a number of poems in French between 1938 and 1939, but in the post-war period the switch was determined and consistent, and Beckett was not to return to writing original work in English for several years. It is from this point on that Beckett truly distinguished himself as a fully bilingual author, translating his own work from French to English and vice versa, often subtly revising or adapting his work in translation (all the published French works of this period also appeared in English after a relatively short period). This is certainly the case for *Waiting for Godot*, and there are a number of differences between the French and English versions. Many of the changes made by Beckett were made in translation, and are a result of the different stylistic and expressive qualities of English, or due to choices made in changing specifically French cultural nuances and references into ones that would be comprehensible to an Anglophone audience. Other changes, such as more specific stage directions and more condensed dialogue, were brought about as a consequence of Beckett's growing experience of working in the theatre, and indeed some were brought about in the rehearsal room (sections struck from the text in the copy used in rehearsals for the premiere of the play, for example, were not translated into English and were cut from subsequent French editions).[3]

Beckett's turn to French in the 1950s seems to have facilitated his development of a very particular perspective on language. A few years earlier, in a letter to a German acquaintance Axel Kaun, Beckett had expressed a hope for a time 'when language is most efficiently used where it is being most efficiently misused', and declared his intention to mount '[a]n assault against words in the name of beauty' (Beckett 1983, 173, 171–2). He had already gone some way towards achieving this aim in English in the novel *Watt*, which marks a significant stylistic break from his densely elusive and erudite earlier work. It is when he begins to write in French, though, that Beckett's unique style really begins to appear, and that he throws off the shackles of the influence of predecessors and contemporaries (most notably James Joyce, who had heavily influenced much of Beckett's early prose). Beckett gave a number of reasons for turning to French, most famously his comment to Niklaus Gessner that French helped him to write 'without style' (Cohn 1973, 58), which critics have usually interpreted as meaning that it enabled him to avoid automatically falling into conventional literary stylistic forms. He once remarked to Richard Coe that the problem with writing in English was that 'you couldn't help writing poetry in it' (Coe 1968, 14). By writing in French first and then translating his own work back into English, Beckett might be seen to be circumventing this impulse in his mother tongue.

This can be seen in *Waiting for Godot*, where Beckett's use of language is irreverent, colloquial, sometimes obscene, and makes use of a more popular range of cultural references than would have been usual in the French, British or Irish theatre traditions. The central characters of the play, after all, are clearly clown-like archetypes, wearing the bowler hats of lovable buffoons such as Charlie Chaplin and Laurel and Hardy, recalling circus antics with their pratfalls and engaging in dialogue which emulates the slick routines of popular vaudeville comedians. All of this was hardly the kind of theatrical vocabulary that had previously been considered worthy of serious drama.

Language in the play is also undermined as a means of conveying information or of signifying the world; dialogue in *Waiting for Godot* refuses to serve to 'flesh out' the characters or to construct a world within which the audience can sustain disbelief. The comic banter of Vladimir and Estragon, for example, fails to provide any substantive information. From what they say we learn next to nothing about them, their environment, their history and precisely whom or what they are waiting for. Instead, their discourse, like the vaudeville routines that it imitates, is playful, pointless, and inconclusive. Its main purpose is, as Vladimir at one point puts it, simply to 'pass the time' (12). Similarly, Lucky's 'thinking' aloud is an enforced performance designed to entertain his master, Pozzo, rather than to provide explanation or enlightenment: his speech presents a deconstruction of rational academic thought and expression into comical and disturbing nonsense. But when Pozzo states that Lucky 'used to think very prettily once' (39), we are led to consider the possibility that Lucky's 'thinking', however coherent it might once have been, was never any more meaningful than it is now. In Act II, the non-referential function of language is even more explicit when Estragon admits that when they keep talking to each other 'It's so we won't think' and 'It's so we won't hear' (62). Language in *Waiting for Godot* is a means of covering up rather than expressing experience.

These particular linguistic preoccupations, which are very much apparent in both the French and subsequent English versions of *Waiting for Godot*, are most fully explored in the other major works produced in the period, which make up the trilogy of novels *Molloy*, *Malone Dies* and *The Unnamable*. Indeed, *Godot* was written in the midst of the trilogy, just after the completion of *Molloy* and *Malone*

*Dies*, and just before the composition of *The Unnamable*. Beckett described this turn to drama as 'a relaxation, to get away from the awful prose I was writing at that time' (Cohn 1987, 138), but the links between the works are more significant than this comment would suggest. *Waiting for Godot* represents not so much an escape from the trilogy as a development of many of the same concerns and themes.

It is impossible to summarize the trilogy in any satisfactory way, in part because these novels all deal in some way with the desire to find meaning and the impossibility of ever doing so. The novels, like the play, resist any neat 'meanings' or definitions that we might try to assign to them. Even the characters that we meet are not presented as stable identities: they tend to mutate, disintegrate, and at times seem to blend into each other (indeed, the narrative voices of these novels make it very difficult to use traditional notions of 'identity' and 'character' as ways of considering what Beckett is expressing). A key concern of these works is the human desire to express – to use language to describe experience, the world, identity – and the inadequacy of language as a means of doing these things. In *Waiting for Godot*, the audience's attention is constantly drawn to the unreliability, the pointlessness or the simple non-referentiality of language; the trilogy is peopled with characters writing 'reports' and telling stories about themselves and others but the veracity of these narratives is consistently undermined. In *Molloy*, for example, the first half of the novel is a 'report' written by the character Molloy which recounts his quest to find his mother, and the second half a 'report' written by another character, Moran, who recounts his failed quest to find Molloy. Both 'reports' purportedly tell their narrators' stories. But Molloy admits that 'even my identity was wrapped in a namelessness often hard to penetrate' (Beckett 1994, 31), complains that 'there could be no things but nameless things, no names but thingless names' (31), and later admits that when he attributes clear language to himself or to others, 'I am merely complying with the convention that demands

you either lie or hold your peace' (87–8). Moran's linguistic degeneration is also significant: he begins with clear succinct language
which refuses to admit any ambiguity, only later to admit: 'Stories,
stories. I have not been able to tell them. I shall not be able to tell
this one' (138), and the end of his narrative explicitly contradicts
its beginning. In the second novel of the trilogy, *Malone Dies*, a
bed-ridden Malone tells himself stories while waiting for death,
stories which are 'calm' and 'almost lifeless, like the teller' (Beckett
1994, 180). In the midst of this 'mortal tedium' (218), Malone is
nonetheless compelled to continue, although he looks forward to
the end of his life and the end of his stories. The tedium of waiting
and Malone's use of language to fill that tedium, and even perhaps
to hasten the end of the wait, are aspects of *Malone Dies* that
are clearly present in *Waiting for Godot*. The inconclusiveness of
Malone's quest for an ending, however, is suggested by the final part
of the trilogy, *The Unnamable*, which is written as a compulsive
stream of speech by a disembodied, unnamable narrator, who is
incapable of finishing his discourse, no matter how much he might
desire to. This third novel problematizes language to such an extent
that the reader is presented with text that is so strange as to be at
times barely comprehensible.

Just as Godot's mysterious authority obliges Vladimir and
Estragon to continue waiting even though he fails to appear, the
protagonists of the trilogy are compelled to continue 'telling' despite
their failure to express: Molloy and Moran write their reports under
the orders of mysterious authority-figures; Malone desires the death
that will come with the end of his narrative, but has to use stories in
order to bring that death and narrative to an end; and the speaker
of the last novel is reduced to a state of unwilling yet constant
verbosity, and an ending which refuses finality:

> [. . .] I can't go on, you must go on, I'll go on, you must say
> words, as long as there are any, until they find me, until they say
> me, strange pain, strange sin, you must go on, perhaps it's done

already, perhaps they have said me already, perhaps they have carried me to the threshold of my story, before the door that opens on my story, that would surprise me, if it opens, it will be I, it will be the silence, where I am, I don't know, I'll never know, in the silence you don't know, you must go on, I can't go on, I'll go on. (Beckett 1994, 418)

Such self-contradictory inconclusiveness is a feature of both the trilogy and *Waiting for Godot*. The unnamable 'can't go on' but nonetheless has to 'go on', and Vladimir and Estragon will never stop waiting: the play's ending juxtaposes Estragon's final line, 'Yes, let's go' with the stage direction '*They do not move*' (94). The individual desire to stop is no match for the compulsion to continue.

## From prose to drama

Considering the trajectory of the trilogy, it is not surprising that Beckett described the turn to drama as a 'relaxation' from his 'awful prose'. This is not to say that the prose was in fact 'awful' – the novels of the trilogy, apart from being considered some of Beckett's greatest work, are also very funny, and *Molloy* and *Malone Dies* in particular contain a similar sort of dark humour as that of *Waiting for Godot*, based on physical degeneration, violence, endless searching or waiting, and the characters' struggles with a range of props. Indeed, these props – including hats, bicycles, sticks and stones – precede the hats and boots that provide so many of the comic routines of *Godot*. But the novels move further and further away from the material world, and hence from such physical humour. By the time we get to *The Unnamable*, the narrative voice is thoroughly disembodied, and language has been rendered so problematic that the only existence of which we can be sure is the existence of the words on the page. With a stage play, however, Beckett could make use of the physical presence of the actors on the stage to create humour, to juxtapose words and action visually (such as in the above example, where the tramps' intention to leave is contradicted by the simple fact of their physical immobility), or to treat the audience to entire comic routines that, taking their cue from direct physicality, do not involve language at all but still express themes of futility or decay. Perhaps Beckett turned to drama simply because, as David Bradby suggests, he 'could expect more of an art form in which language is not the only means of communication' (Bradby 2001, 15). Indeed, Beckett's work from *Waiting for Godot* onwards increasingly experiments with non-verbal means of expression: only a few years after *Godot*, he wrote two mimes, *Act Without Words I* and *II* (both 1956) which present silent human figures caught in desperate and unrelenting environments or routines. He also begins to explore the possibilities of radio: his plays, *All that Fall* (1956) and *Embers* (1959) experiment with non-verbal sound effects, and manipulate the singular impact of silence which can be attained in the pure sound-world of radio. Later, he became interested in other visual media, writing for film in 1963 (the work was called simply *Film* and starred Buster Keaton) and television (*Eh Joe* in 1965 and *Ghost Trio* in 1975 for example). An interest that was particularly significant and enduring for him was music, and later radio plays such as *Words and Music* (1961) and *Cascando* (1962) directly pit words against the expressive potential of music.

The great success of *Waiting for Godot* may also have influenced Beckett's decision to continue to write for the theatre. In engaging with rehearsals, too, he may have recognized that a theatrical medium offered different opportunities for controlling the reception and experience of his work. A reader is free to read the book anywhere and at any speed, to refer back or forwards to other parts of the text, and to draw conclusions about the central meaning and significance of the text at his or her leisure. An audience, on the other hand, experiences a play in a specific place and for a specific length of time as governed by the author and director, and consumes information in a paced, linear manner. Beckett can be seen to have made the most of this quality of theatre in *Waiting for Godot*. It is a play which refuses to 'say' anything in terms of delivering an interpretable 'message' but which, instead, makes its audience experience the very issues it addresses. Of course, a key aspect of our experience of the play, which fiction or poetry could not satisfactorily provide, is the experience of being made to wait for explanations and for dramatic resolutions which never arrive. Usually, within the first moments of a play, we look for clarification of what is going on by investing in characters, by presuming that they will clarify their situation and their motivations. Our investments usually reap rewards, and we latch our interest onto the fates of the characters being played out in front of us. Within what we learn, we try to consider the value of different props, actions, gestures, elements of dialogue, and come to ready conclusions that permit us to process the information as it is given to us within a narrative constructed of a series of logical causes and effects. Beckett overturned such presumptions with *Waiting for Godot* and our investments in his characters fail to provide any coherent sense, or any conclusive results. The focus of our waiting in the first instance, just like that of the two men on stage, is the character of Godot. We are led to think that all will be clear when this character arrives on stage, but that investment is worn thin as the character fails to show his face. When the second act begins as though from the beginning, we perhaps too feel we 'can't go on', but remain seated all the same. When Estragon complains that 'Nothing happens, nobody comes, nobody goes, it's awful!' (41), he is echoing our tense experience of the play from the stalls. We too are waiting for something meaningful to happen.

In the persistent absence of any answers, explanations, or even any discernable plot, we clutch at the apparently pointless comic routines and idle banter as our entertainment, just as the characters employ them to pass the time. And each time Pozzo and Lucky appear on the scene, the cruelty and brutality inherent in their relationship (in Act I), and their comical physical decrepitude (in Act II) become as much a relief from the monotony of nothing happening for us as it is for Vladimir and Estragon. Lucky's speech is as much 'entertainment' for us (and it can, indeed, be extremely funny) as it has been for Pozzo, and in these ways Beckett implicates the spectator in the brutality of the master–slave relationship. He brings the experience of the audience closer to the experience of his characters, perhaps even encouraging us to consider the possibility that our very presence in the theatre might be just another way of 'passing the time' and of filling the void while waiting for whatever our own lives will bring. As audience we ultimately fail to know, to achieve assurance, and the characters and situation of the play do not end in any resolution of the dilemmas it presents. Beckett therefore makes us hope for resolution and feel frustration at its not being provided. This is precisely the quality of human existence and aspiration that, arguably, he was trying to capture. Only the theatrical genre could effectively offer such an experience and Beckett was the first dramatic author to harness that potential to powerful effect.

Beckett's turn to drama, then, can be seen as a way of finding a more effective means of making an audience experience his art and drawing their attention away from the instinct to attempt to 'understand' it on an intellectual level. The drive to 'understand' is a relationship to 'meaning' that prose is more likely to promote and permit in the reflective reader. Beckett's writing consistently and persistently resists such 'understanding', and he refused ever to provide answers or explanations. He once told a group of students that:

> I want neither to instruct nor improve nor to keep people from getting bored. I want to bring poetry into drama, a poetry which has been through the void and makes a new start in a new room-space. I think in new dimensions and basically am not

very worried about whether I can be followed. I couldn't give the answers that were hoped for. There are no easy solutions. (Knowlson 1997, 477)

Beckett's trilogy of novels attempted to convey such uncertainty and ambiguity, while simultaneously attempting to undermine the very means (language) by which it can do this. *Waiting for Godot*, however, manages to get beyond this aporia by creating an affective experience for the audience that is not purely linguistic.

## *Waiting for Godot* and theatrical traditions

In France, the popular theatre of the pre- and post-war stage was still very much dominated by the commercial model of late nineteenth-century Parisian theatre, which was heavily reliant on the celebrity draw of a handful of famous actors and writers to attract audiences, much as Hollywood or Bollywood films today invest importance in the casting of recognized stars to ensure box-office success. In such an environment, the artistic value of a script was not a currency that paid dividends. The old formulae of writers such as Eugène Labiche, Victorien Sardou and Eugène Scribe still ruled the day in the boulevard theatres, where the so-called 'well-made play' (one that developed a narrative from opening exposition, through development of a crisis, climax, and denouement to a happy or tragic conclusion) held fast. In his *The Theatre and its Double*, published in 1938, the French poet, actor and performance theorist Antonin Artaud bemoaned the state of the Paris theatre, complained that 'everything that is not contained in dialogue [. . .] has been left in the background' (Artaud 1993, 26) and questioned tradition by asking 'whoever said theatre was made to define character, to resolve conflicts of a human, emotional order, of a present-day, psychological nature'? (31)

Post-war theatres in Britain were run as commercial enterprises, with output controlled by management groups more interested in their bottom line than fresh ideas. Unlike in Paris, where small private theatres grew and disappeared like mushrooms in the dark alleyways of the Left Bank, there was no experimental London fringe. There were still no nationally subsidized theatres and the new Arts Council's policies did nothing to encourage or support new writing. Variety acts of song and dance and comedy accounted for a third of all theatrical revenue, cinema was on the rise and television came into its own as the great popular entertainer in the mid-1950s. Between the end of the war and the arrival of *Waiting for Godot* in London in 1955, the number of companies playing theatrical repertoires had more than halved. Those that survived gave audiences a steady and safe diet of 'well-made' plays from the pens of writers such as Agatha Christie, Noel Coward, J. B. Priestley, Terence Rattigan and Peter Ustinov. Samuel Beckett's *Waiting for Godot* mounted the first serious challenge to this state of affairs. The task of creating forums within which a new avant-garde might flourish was soon after taken up by the English Stage Theatre by promoting an innovative, writer-driven agenda at the Royal Court Theatre.

Though Beckett claimed to have no interest in going to the theatre, his innovative drama did not come from nowhere. He certainly had no practical experience of making theatre when he wrote his first drama, with the exception of having played a role in a skit on Pierre Corneille's *Le Cid*, entitled *Le Kid* (invoking Chaplin), as a twenty-five-year-old lecturer at Trinity College, Dublin in 1931. This amateur fun aside, Beckett was a stranger to the rehearsal room until he bemusedly witnessed Blin at work in the winter months of 1952. Nonetheless, he had maintained an interest in drama from a young age: frequenting theatres had always been a part of his cultural diet, despite any later denial, and he was well read on classic and contemporary dramatic literature. His love of Jean Racine's drama *Andromaque* (1667), for example, might be discernable in *Waiting for Godot*: for all its revolutionary structure, Beckett's play respects the classical trinity of unities of time, place and narrative, and like Racine's eponymous heroine, the protagonists of Beckett's drama await a fate over which they have no control, and must accept meagre scraps of information offered by messengers. The plays of John Millington Synge that Beckett saw at the Abbey Theatre in Dublin as a young man were also a significant influence. The manner in which Synge merged laughter with pathos, expressed a philosophical pessimism and offered precise imagery are all characteristic of Beckett's own writing.

Despite the difficulties that Beckett experienced in getting his play produced there, Paris was in many ways the ideal location for its lengthy birth. In the mid-twentieth century, the French capital was an unparalleled centre of artistic and cultural activity, and a fertile breeding ground for experimentation in theatrical presentation. The Dada movement had transplanted itself in Paris from Zurich after the First World War and brought with it exciting and brash innovations in the composition and physical presentation of poetry. Tristan Tzara, one of the main proponents of the movement, was a supporter of *Waiting for Godot* and was instrumental in enthusing Roger Blin, the play's first director, into taking on the project. The outrageous provocations of the Dadaists had in turn inspired the Surrealist movement, which comprised authors such as Antonin Artaud, Jean Cocteau and Roger Vitrac. Surrealistic drama such as Artaud's parody *The Spurt of Blood* (1924) or Cocteau's *Orpheus* (1926) shocked and provoked audiences with audacious imagery, non-logical narratives and behaviour that challenged or ridiculed middle-class attitudes, beliefs or behaviour. For all the controversy that such material might arouse, the Parisian cultural scene could sustain and maintain a healthy stream of innovators and artistic renewal in ways that London or Dublin could not offer. The fringe and experimental theatres in Paris also offered a forum within which an accepted wisdom that the author was a key progenitor of theatrical reform and innovation prevailed. Elsewhere, the power of the actor-manager had perhaps too strong a stranglehold on artistic policy. In coming to ground in the creative backwaters of the Parisian avant-garde, *Waiting for Godot* was brought into the world in a fertile and supportive environment.

## Beckett after Godot

*Waiting for Godot* thrust its author into a literary celebrity the consequences of which (demands for interviews, the award of honours, academic speculation) he spent the rest of his life doing his best to avoid. James Knowlson's *Damned to Fame* has the perfect title for a biography of a celebrated writer who sought and cherished solitude and a simple, uncluttered lifestyle. As his most famous play was enjoying its extended run in Paris in 1953, Beckett had a modest, two-roomed house built on a small plot of land he bought just outside the rural village of Ussy-sur-Marne and he spent the rest of his life divided between a calm, remote existence there and his apartment in Paris, where he maintained a base with his wife to be able to conduct the various meetings that came along with the details of publication and production of his works. After *Waiting for Godot*, he went on to pen a further nineteen dramas, seven radio plays, five television screenplays, one film and numerous prose outputs. Of his other theatre writing, *Endgame* (1957) and *Happy Days* (1962) are the most well known and continue his vision of a bleak existence in which the individual seeks to avoid contemplation of the conditions of their existence. The self-absorbed, blind Hamm bossing the lame, subjected Clov in *Endgame* are reminiscent of the Pozzo and Lucky couple, and together with Hamm's legless parents, kept inside dustbins, they live a daily domestic routine of torment, recrimination and waiting. The character of Winnie in *Happy Days*, stuck up to her waist in a hole in the ground, merrily witters away her time as though in perpetual denial of her evident state of physical and mental decay, and the fate that awaits her, brought all the more distinctly to our attention in the second act, in which she is reduced to a mere head sticking out of the ground. This image of bodily dysfunction and destruction featured heavily in Beckett's subsequent drama, from the three heads in urns rapidly recounting their interrelated narratives in *Play* (1963), to the head suspended in the dark in *That Time* (1975) or just a mouth talking incessantly in the void, as in *Not I* (1972). Some of the final words of his last dramatic work, *What Where* (1983), might be deemed a suitable epilogue to his entire output: 'Time passes. That is all. Make sense who may' (Beckett 1986, 476). He was awarded the Nobel Prize for Literature in 1969, and, though he was flattered by the honour, his immediate reaction was one of distress and fear at the disruption to his daily routines the media attention would cause. Too timid and self-effacing to make a public appearance to accept the award, he sent his publisher Jérôme Lindon to Stockholm to accept on his behalf. Typical of his generosity, he made gifts of the award to support other artists. Beckett died in 1989, leaving behind a remarkable bilingual portfolio of fiction and drama that has had a significant impact upon both anglophone and francophone literary and theatrical traditions.

# 2 Analysis and Commentary

## What is it about?

If you are reading this book, it is perhaps because you are hopeful – out of studious necessity or casual enthusiasm – that it will offer you an easily digestible explanation of this most enigmatic of plays, or that it will provide you with clarifications of its various mysteries. While we are striving to offer a map over the terrain of the drama and to provide an accessible key to that map, it might be useful before we attempt to do so to halt and consider that very appetite that you are hopeful we might satisfy.

It is a human trait to require answers and clarification; we prefer to believe that we have the measure of things around us, of our experience, of ourselves, of the real dilemmas that we encounter daily, rather than to accept that these things are often beyond our comprehension and ready control. We nonetheless often achieve and maintain a belief of control or perspective, even if this means living in denial of demonstrable truths. The one absolute certainty in our life, for example, is that it will end one day, but we collectively need to keep that fact out of our minds in order to get on with things. As we have seen, the project of much of Beckett's *oeuvre* involves the very scrutiny of that human drive for clarification: his work insistently reminds us of those truths which we would rather forget, such as the brevity of life and the inevitability of death, and refuses to provide the sorts of answers we want. It makes sense, then, that Beckett himself consistently refused to explain the play to audiences, critics, friends or scholars.

In 1952, when the director Roger Blin was trying to procure funding to be able to convince a theatre manager to risk staging this obscure play by a playwright known only for his dense, literary novels, he had a few of the play's scenes recorded and performed over the airwaves of RTF (Radiodiffusion-Télévision Française). The idea of this, technically the first public performance of the play, was to garner some publicity for it. Beckett agreed to write a frontispiece, which Blin read out before the extracts were played. It is the longest example of him holding forth on the play and worth quoting in full:

> You ask me what I think about *Waiting for Godot* – extracts from which you do me the honour of presenting on the Club d'Essai – and at the same time you ask for my views on the theatre. I have no views on the theatre. I know nothing about it. I never go. There is nothing wrong with that. What is no doubt less acceptable is, first of all, to write a play under these conditions and then, having written it, not to have any views about it either. That, unfortunately, is the case for me. Not everybody is capable of moving calmly from the world which unfolds on the page to the world of profit-and-loss and back again, just as a worker might go between his workplace and the Café du Commerce. I know no more about this play than anybody who might manage to read it carefully. I do not know in what spirit I wrote it. I do not know any more about the characters than what they say, what they do, and what happens to them. Of their appearance, I had to describe what little I could perceive. Their bowler hats, for example. I do not know who Godot is. I do not even know if he exists – especially not that. And I do not know if they believe in him or not, the two men who are waiting for him. As for the other two who pass by towards the end of both Acts, that must be to break the monotony. Everything I could have known,

I have shown. It is not much. But it is enough for me, amply enough. I would even go so far as to say that I would have been content with less. As for wanting to find in it all a broader, loftier meaning for the audience to carry away from the performance along with their programmes and choc-ices, I really cannot see the point. But it must be possible. I am not in that world any more and I never will be again. Estragon, Vladimir, Pozzo, Lucky, their time and their space – I was able to get to know them a little but only from the perspective of not needing to understand. They owe you something, perhaps. Let them sort things out themselves. Without me. They and I are done with each other. (Trincal 1994, 2)[1]

Here, on the occasion of the play's first public incarnation, its author quite deliberately distances himself from any presumed responsibility to explain what *Waiting for Godot* is 'about'. He maintained this stance throughout his life in relation to all his writing. Later, for example, when his American director Alan Schneider asked him the question any student of the play wishes first to pose, 'Who or what does Godot mean?', he answered 'If I knew, I would have said so in the play' (Calder 1967, 38). It is important to put this kind of response into perspective: it is not a deliberately obtuse position that Beckett adopts, but a straightforwardly honest one. He does not know who Godot is, because that which Godot might represent is not one single entity, identity or experience, but a collection of such things that all imply the same condition of being. This chapter will offer a ready anatomy of the play by considering the characters, the narrative, the style and structure, but in doing so we recognize and emphasize that we cannot find, and you should not be encouraged to look for, simple definitive responses to the meaning of a play which addresses that very appetite to find meaning.

## Responses to character

The play's principal personages, Vladimir and Estragon, are not typical theatrical characters. They stand before us on stage and offer us no clear indication of their past, of how they met, and what brought them to the state of destitution in which we see them. The popular response to these two characters is to perceive them as tramps. Beckett himself never specified this, although their itinerant past, their lack of substantial food, and their tendency to beg and scavenge for scraps would suggest a vagrant existence. We are also offered glimpses of some former more dignified existence, in Estragon's self-mocking reference to the rags he wears (12) or in Vladimir's reverie of a joint suicide bid: 'Hand in hand from the top of the Eiffel Tower, among the first. We were respectable in those days. Now it's too late. They wouldn't even let us up' (10). Bereft of exposition, the play opens with these two characters greeting each other (presumably after waking one morning having slept in the open), grumbling about their afflictions, discussing the Bible and announcing that they cannot leave the spot because they are waiting for someone called Godot. We learn scant else about them subsequently, and what we do know of them is gleaned from their behaviour more than from what they say.

In his original handwritten manuscript, Beckett gave his principal characters the names of Vladimir and Levy, renaming Levy as Estragon by the time he got to drafting the second act. The surname Levy was so commonplace in French Jewish communities that it was virtually synonymous with 'Jewish' to French audiences, just as 'Smith' or 'Dupont' might respectively suggest representative Anglo-Saxon or Gallic ethnicities. Beckett, who had experienced the loss of close Jewish friends to Nazi concentration camps, perhaps rejected the overtly Jewish name in preference for a name that might be more broadly representative, or which avoided any indication of a specific history of human suffering such as the Holocaust. Estragon is the French word for the herb Tarragon, and is never usually employed as a person's name. Perhaps the name serves to associate its character with the soil, the earth to which he is attracted to sit and sleep, and with the kind of scant nourishment that the characters gain intellectually and emotionally (herbs in themselves provide flavour but little nutrition).

Of the two tramps' names, only Estragon's is announced during the play, and only once, by Vladimir when recounting his day (90). Vladimir's name exists only in the printed programme to any production, though he is addressed as 'Mister Albert', by Godot's young messenger (49). The names we associate most with these two principal characters, as they are the appellations most frequently used in the play, are the diminutives Didi (Vladimir) and Gogo (Estragon). These suggest both a familiarity and childishness that the couple share. They also sound like clowns' names, as do the other two-syllable names Pozzo, Lucky and Godot. Ruby Cohn points out that the diminutive names also point towards the two men's dispositions; Estragon's attachment to the earth and the bodily (go go) and Vladimir's predilection for reflection and philosophy (dis dis – in French 'say say') (Cohn 1965, 171). Another referent that the names Didi and Gogo draw on is the id and the ego coupling in Sigmund Freud's structural theory, in which the id is the unconscious element of the human psyche which contains repressed memories and emotions and the ego is the conscious part which engages with external reality. While it would be fatuous to attempt to equate Vladimir and Estragon with the id and the ego as a means better to understand them – such an exercise would presume Beckett had embodied them thus, and there is little evidence of that – it is attractive to consider them as containing bound but opposing, mutually complementary characteristics, thereby representing human impulses more forcefully as a pair, a unit, than as separate characters.

This mutuality is certainly something that Beckett's own *mise en scène* emphasized, for example, in the costume choices for the characters (see p. 70), and embedded in the play are numerous oppositions that the two perform. Vladimir is clearly the thinker, the philosopher, the intellectual of the two, while Estragon is more concerned with bodily comfort, including sleep and food. As with his name, the root vegetables which comprise his diet tie him to the earth, and he frequently seeks repose and respite on the ground. Vladimir, by contrast, is drawn to the tree, reaching upward to the sky. This difference between the two men is captured figuratively in Estragon's business with his boots and Vladimir's with his hat, both scratching around inside their respective sources of irritation. Beckett referred to this as the 'Hat Boot analogy' and, in German, opted to refer to Estragon's boots as 'Dreckschuhe' (mud shoes), further tying the character with the earth (Knowlson 1993, 95). On a more vulgar level, Estragon's feet stink while Vladimir's halitosis has him smelling from the organ associated with speech and expression. When Pozzo asks for requests, Estragon wants Lucky to dance (the physical) whereas Vladimir is interested to hear him think (the intellectual).

The critic Vivian Mercier once pointed out to Beckett that he had made Vladimir and Estragon sound erudite, as though they had PhDs. 'How do you know they hadn't?' came the reply (Brater 2003, 75). Some former intellectual capacity and engagement is certainly evident in Vladimir, and its obvious failure is a key strain in the motif of entropy that frames the play. In the play's first moments, he partially quotes from the Bible, forgetting the source, and later remembers the occult writings on the relationship between mandrakes and ejaculate of hanged men. He quotes from Thomas Aquinas and William Shakespeare, and even sometimes speaks in pentameters. Estragon, by contrast, is the poet fallen on harder times, something he directly alludes to in half-jest. In the French and German texts, and in an earlier English version of the text, he refers to himself as Catullus, the Roman poet,[2] and contorts Percy Bysshe Shelley's 'To the Moon' with his 'Pale for weariness [. . .] Of climbing heaven and gazing on the likes of us' (52) and Shakespeare's Polonius with his 'We are all born mad. Some remain so' (80). While Vladimir is intellectual, and capable of wistfully going off on quasi-philosophical soliloquies on his tiresome waiting, Estragon is practically equipped, and it is he, for example, who has to explain to Vladimir the risks involved in the heavier of the two hanging himself first on the meagre tree branch (17–18). In such subtle ways, Beckett demonstrates both the waning of the intellect, and its diminished effectiveness in responding to the needs of existence. He also makes the two men's interdependence all the more clear to us.

As with Vladimir and Estragon, Pozzo and Lucky are a complementary pair bound together (literally in this case, by a rope) as an interdependent unit. The character of Pozzo is brutish and self-absorbed from the off. He seems almost to have been written as a set of characteristics that one might associate with a vain, wealthy bourgeois: he is corpulent, bossy and self-important. The word 'pozzo' is Italian for a well, a deep hole, but may have been chosen for no other reason than its phonic similarity to Godot (to permit Didi and Gogo's initial optimistic misunderstanding), to sustain the two-syllable convention, and to sound clown-like as those other names do. In choosing an Italian sounding name, Beckett also effectively reduced any ability easily to locate the play, suggesting instead a generic wilderness that was at once Slavic (Vladimir), Gallic (Estragon), Anglo-Saxon (Lucky) and Roman (Pozzo). The similarity to the Italian 'pazzo' (madman) is also perhaps resonant, engaging with the character's delusions of self-worth that are seen as no more than a collection of lifestyle trappings that fail ultimately to protect him from decay and torment. As a punitive figure who demands attention and respect, he is also something of a parody of Godliness, and we might infer the notion of humans being made in God's image in his declaration that Vladimir and Estragon are 'Of the same species as Pozzo!' (23).

As his manservant, Lucky represents an aspect of Pozzo's upper-middle-class trappings. Here, the master/servant relationship is expressed quite severely, with Lucky being treated like an animal and kept on the end of a leash. Beckett originally envisaged Lucky dressed as a railway porter, emphasizing his institutionalized servitude (Taylor-Batty 2007, 106). Whereas Pozzo indulges in bodily pleasures, such as eating and smoking, Lucky is able to express intellectual and aesthetic pursuits (such as his monolithic 'think' and his less impressive dance) though his competence in these things is not what it once was. Like Didi and Gogo, this new pair seem to be split between body and mind, with the decaying and unreliable distractions of the intellect no longer able to distract the physical body from its appetites and disrepair. This is clear with Pozzo's reaction to the 'think' and is further accentuated in Act Two when Pozzo returns incapacitated by blindness and Lucky mute. Beckett in this way represents the human mind as inarticulate and unable to lead the incapacitated flesh. 'The Beckettian mind or spirit' David Pattie succinctly clarifies, 'is, in Yeats' resonant phrase, "tethered to a dying animal." It is condemned to observe an inevitable process of decay, in which it is powerless to intervene' (Oppenheim 2004, 231).

Lucky's moniker is, at first glance, ironic: there is seemingly nothing lucky about his circumstances. Fated to carry the weighty accessories of his master, at his beck and call, insulted and derided, expected to dance or recite at whim, held at humiliating distance by a chafing rope around his neck, Lucky seems to be the least fortunate of the play's quartet of main characters. And yet, perhaps this irony is an indicator to the play's thematic thrust, and therefore something of a clue. Of all four, only Lucky has found a position that offers him some sense of satisfaction, or comfort even. He even violently defends his own subjugation, kicking Estragon when he attempts to console him (32). Perhaps, even in his tethers, or because of them, he has a position in the world which is knowable, consistent and patterned. Indeed, Lucky was, for Beckett, perhaps the 'luckiest' character of the play: 'I suppose he is lucky to have no more expectations', he told Colin Duckworth (lxiii). The other characters covet an existence like Lucky's that is knowable and free from unsatiated waiting, and even the news that Godot, like Pozzo, can act violently towards his servants does not diminish Vladimir and Estragon's keenness to make their rendezvous and enter his service.

All four characters wear bowler hats, and this was something that Beckett insisted upon. The bowler hat was originally designed in the 1850s for huntsmen and groundsmen as a reinforced, practical and more protective version of the upper-class top hat. In the early twentieth century it was associated with both servility, as the common headgear of gentlemen's valets, and middle-class probity, being the apparel of white-collar workers such as lawyers, bankers and civil servants. It was the hat of choice of the famous comic performers Stan Laurel and Oliver Hardy, as well as an essential ingredient in the image of the tramp figure created by Charlie Chaplin in films such as *The Kid* (1921) and *Modern Times* (1936). Beckett enjoyed early screen comedies such as these, and one can note in *Godot* homage perhaps being paid to timeless comedy routines such as Laurel and Hardy's struggle with boots in *Be Big* (1930) or the Marx Brothers *lazzi* of swapping hats around in *Duck Soup* (1933). In such classic screen humour, the bowler hat sheltered the impoverished or simple characters the comedians created beneath a fragile glaze of middle-class respectability. It symbolized their aspiration towards social integration and acceptance, and was therefore a constant comic or pathos-ridden reminder of their inadequacies and failures to achieve those objectives. The iconic image of Stan Laurel removing his hat to scratch his head in bewilderment captures the amusing tension between comic human frailty and the pathetic aspiration to disguise or deny that frailty. This head scratching is emulated, of course, by both Vladimir and Estragon in Beckett's play.

## Narrative structures

One cannot speak of *Waiting for Godot* having a 'plot' or 'story' in the conventional sense. It is a play in which 'nothing happens, twice', as critic Vivian Mercier sardonically noted (Mercier 1956, 6) or, in Estragon's words '[n]othing happens, nobody comes, nobody goes, it's awful' (41). The play was revolutionary precisely because Beckett recognized what was ordinarily expected by spectators of a play and subverted those expectations, and to specific effect. Having characters onstage who talk of being there to wait for a man called Godot would suggest that the character Godot is eventually going to arrive and bring about the kind of resolution, happy or tragic, that we might usually expect an evening at the theatre to provide. Instead, we too are kept waiting, and we too are denied the resolution that Godot's arrival might bring the two tramps. We are not invited to consider the play's themes. To be invited to consider a theme is to accept that some solution or conclusion might be drawn.

Of course, it is not altogether true to say that nothing happens in the play. Estragon and Vladimir pass the time in chatter and games, Pozzo and Lucky arrive, Pozzo deliberates, Lucky 'thinks', Pozzo and Lucky leave and a boy arrives to announce that Godot will arrive on the morrow. The second act repeats the sequence of events, with Pozzo and Lucky in a deteriorated state. Both acts end with the same exchange between Vladimir and Estragon: 'Well, shall we go?' 'Yes, let's go', and the same instruction '*They do not move*', the exchange being initiated first by one and then the other (54 and 93). As throughout the whole play, any impetus to move, to change the situation, is deadened, overwhelmed by the hope that Godot will, one day, arrive. And so the events of waiting and passing the time are ordained to begin all over again. In this way, we are invited to think that perhaps these two days are two of a sequence of never-ending, ever-repeating days. Estragon complains that 'Nothing happens, nobody comes, nobody goes' (41), but it is in fact more a case of pretty much the same sort of thing happening every day, and the same people coming and going. In each Act, the arrival of Pozzo and Lucky is initially mistaken for Godot's arrival and thus brings hope. Their departure, however, brings no change to the existence of Vladimir and Estragon, apart from having provided some variation on the boredom of waiting. In effect, things happen, but nothing changes, except by degrees for the worse.

Like Vladimir's endlessly repeating song at the beginning of Act II (57–8), much of the repetition in *Waiting for Godot* is circular: the end of each day brings the characters round to the beginning of the next day, but each beginning merely starts the whole process all over again. The structure of the play is founded on repetition – of words, events, motifs, sequences of movement – and it operates like a musical score in that respect, stating and restating its themes in a series of ever so slightly varied verbal and gestural leitmotifs. Such repetitions are too numerous to list, and most are self-evident, but it is worth noting the subtle pairings that are attached to these repetitions, such as Estragon's investigation of his boots (11) matching Vladimir's investigation inside his hat (10–11), or Vladimir's stinking breath offsetting Estragon's stinking feet.

Ultimately, what we witness in *Waiting for Godot* – and what we are invited to experience – is time being negotiated, filled, passed. Vladimir and Estragon employ a large variety of strategies to pass the time: idle banter, speculation, telling jokes (a risky business for Vladimir, given his inability to control his bladder when laughing), playing language games, falling asleep, contemplating suicide, eating, contradicting or insulting one another. When Pozzo and Lucky arrive they are referred to, with a wry meta-theatrical wink to the audience's tested patience, as 'reinforcements' (77) and they too are used as a means of distraction in their absence, when Vladimir suggests to Estragon that they play at imitating the master/slave couple (72–3). Such games and distractions serve an important purpose for Vladimir and Estragon, not because they are in any way significant, but precisely because of their insignificance: at one point, in the midst of an argument over radishes, turnips and carrots, Vladimir complains 'This is becoming really insignificant', to which

Estragon replies 'Not enough' (68). Such activities, just like the popular forms of entertainment that the play draws upon, are escapist pastimes for 'relaxation' and 'recreation' (69). Estragon, however, hints at a more significant function of such play: 'We always find something, eh Didi, to give us the impression we exist?' (69) They cannot bear silence, they cannot bear the inaction of waiting that corroborates the emptiness of their actual existence. Vladimir's impatient answer to Estragon's revelation, however, emphasizes the superficial trickery involved in their games: 'Yes, yes, we're magicians.' As Vladimir declares, 'habit is a great deadener' (91), suggesting his awareness that the strategies they use to pass the daylight hours are so much anaesthetic to dull the pain of their waiting, of their being there.

## Modernism or Postmodernism

The narrative structures outlined above are a crucial aspect of Beckett's theatrical innovation. In refusing the traditional tenets of the 'well-made play', he is also refusing the siphons of meaning that such a structure imposes on a play. Traditional character, plot development (logical chronology and progression), and the finality of narrative resolution are all, for Beckett, artificial constructs which artists use to represent reality, but which in fact distort reality. In this regard, Beckett was continuing the legacy of those early twentieth-century writers whom we now term 'modernist' – writers like James Joyce, Virginia Woolf, T. S. Eliot, and Marcel Proust – who felt the need to develop new and innovative ways of representing the modern world. For modernist writers, as for Beckett, to provide such a clear structure is to obscure the complex, chaotic, illogical and constantly changing experience of life which most people call 'reality'. As Woolf, for example, writes in her essay 'Modern Fiction': 'if a writer were a free man and not a slave, if he could write what he chose, not what he must, if he could base his work upon his own feeling and not upon convention, there would be no plot, no comedy, no tragedy, no love interest or catastrophe in the accepted style, and perhaps not a single button sewn on as the Bond Street tailors would have it' (Woolf 2003, 150). But this is not to say that modernist writing is formless; indeed, it is quite the opposite: modernist writers, while rejecting traditional forms, construct their own new, unique, but nonetheless carefully formalized works of art. Beckett echoes this typically modernist concern in the following words to Tom Driver:

> What I am saying does not mean that there will henceforth be no form in art. It only means that there will be new form, and that this form will be of such a type that it admits the chaos, and does not try to say that the chaos is really something else. The form and the chaos remain separate. The latter is not reduced to the former. That is why the form itself becomes a preoccupation, because it exists as a problem separate from the material it accommodates. To find a form that accommodates the mess, that is the task of the artist. (Driver 1961, 23)

The narrative structure of *Waiting for Godot* constitutes one example of Beckett's attempt to 'find a form that accommodates the mess': the patterns, repetitions and variations and narrative circularity of the play are all very carefully constructed to resist narrative resolution and any attempt by the audience to impose meaning upon the play. Essentially, the form of *Godot* is designed to make the play, like the tramps, go nowhere. The form itself is elegant and minimalist, stripped down to a few emblematic gestures and phrases.

Modernist principles also invaded theatre practice, and on the French stage authors such as Alfred Jarry, Guillaume Apollinaire, Jean Cocteau and Antonin Artaud had striven in the early decades of the last century to subvert stage naturalism and the theatre of dialogue by recommending a 'poetry of the stage' of 'moving hiero-glyphs.'[3] In other words, these playwrights rejected traditional realist forms of representation in favour of attempts to promote an affective stage language derived from gesture, rhythm, colour, move-ment and pace. Inventing the word 'surrealism' to define the process of lucid poetic imagery of association that he had seen in Cocteau's theatrical innovation, Apollinaire stated that 'when man wanted to imitate walking he created the wheel, which does not resemble a leg' (Schumacher 1984, 147). His argument was that in capturing the purpose and essence of an idea, it can be more efficient to think beyond realistic representation. When Beckett insisted (in relation to the religious references to being saved or damned in his play) that he was 'interested in the shape of ideas even if I do not believe them' and that 'it's the shape that matters' (Hobson 1956, 153) he was perhaps echoing Apollinaire's ethos and wishing to draw attention to the expressivity and affect of form over the prevailing realist presumption that content, 'message' or mechanical representation, can legitimately capture and convey human experience. This relates to Beckett's view on language as a conveyor of meaning. As we indi-cated in Chapter 1, Beckett felt that language could never be renewed or redeemed, and that consequently 'to be an artist is to fail, as no other dare fail' (Beckett, 1983: 145). This is why Beckett does not talk about representing 'chaos': for him, representing something in art is simply impossible.

It is in Beckett's very modernist attempt to 'find a form that accommodates the mess' that he begins to depart from modernism and starts to approach what is known as postmodernism, however. Writers like Proust, Woolf, and Joyce might all have written works that were extremely innovative, but they all retained a sense of there being some kind of 'reality' that could be represented, and of individual subjective perspectives from which that 'reality' could be viewed. They might have bent and stretched language to experi-mental extremes, and they might have expressed suspicion of language's effectiveness, but they nonetheless believed in the ability of new literary forms (and in some cases new literary languages) to represent the world. We should also note that Beckett refers, not to the chaotic nature of life or of our perception of the world (as Woolf does in the above quotation), but to 'the chaos': life, experience, identity – everything – is formless. A particular aspect of *Waiting for Godot* which critics have interpreted as a shift from a modernist attitude towards postmodernism is the way Beckett questions and undermines the ideologies that we construct and the stories that we tell ourselves in order to assign 'meaning' or 'purpose' to our existence.

According to the theorist Jean-François Lyotard, writing in 1979, postmodernism is characterized by the loss of 'grand narratives'.[4] 'Grand narratives', as Simon Malpas writes, 'produce systematic accounts of how the world works, how it develops over history, and the place of human beings within it. Put simply, grand narratives construct accounts of human society and progress' (Malpas 2005, 37). Now, *Waiting for Godot* presents us with a world where such explanations and narratives of progress are either absent or ineffectual. The tramps do not seem to know what they are waiting for, they do nothing useful, and they make no progress. The only ostensible reason for being there is, of course, the possible arrival of Godot. We might even say that Godot forms the very basis of Vladimir and Estragon's existence in the play: the idea of Godot, and the hope that accompanies that idea, underlies everything they do, where they stay, how they behave. As Vladimir puts it, 'in this immense confusion one thing alone is clear. We are waiting for Godot to come' (80). It is not clear what Godot would actually do if he came, and neither Vladimir nor Estragon seem to know anything about him. In Act II, Vladimir quizzes the boy about him, but gleans very little information: he has a white beard, apparently, and 'does nothing' (91). Nonetheless, all their hopes and dreams rest on his arrival: Vladimir's triumphant cry when he thinks Godot is finally coming is 'It's Godot! At last! Gogo! It's Godot! We're saved!' (73). Godot is their belief, their salvation, their ideology, and therefore, in postmodern terms, their 'grand narrative'. But Godot is conspicuous not only for his absence and his failure to turn up, but for his absolute indeterminacy: he is unknown and unknowable for both protagonists and for audience. Indeed, he might not exist at all. It is very important that we do not attempt to assign meaning to Godot, or even to assert his meaninglessness (for even to do that is paradoxically to assign him a meaning in the play). The point is, Godot constitutes an absent and unknowable idea, which fails to explain or have any positive effect on their lives, but which nonetheless governs their existence. Beckett, in this play, can therefore be seen to undermine the notion of any idea that keeps us going, that we use to explain or give meaning to our existence. In short, *Waiting for Godot* undermines our subscription to and dependence upon 'grand narratives'.

*Waiting for Godot* is interesting because it is a transitional text: it still manifests many of the concerns of modernism, but starts to question the implied stability of those concerns, and shows the signs of Beckett's later move towards more explicitly postmodernist forms of indeterminacy. Take characterization, for example. The notion of a stable self developing and changing through time, gaining knowledge and wisdom along the way, is a 'grand narrative' which forms the basis of traditional literary and theatrical characterization, and which is also very much present in modernist literature. *Waiting for Godot* goes some way to challenging this 'grand narrative' by refusing to provide us with 'fully rounded' and 'realistic' characters, but it does still provide characters who are recognizable and stable enough for us to have been able to provide the above character summaries. Beckett's later works are much more radical in this regard, often challenging the very basis of our notions of identity and subjectivity by systematically undermining the notion of a stable self (as is made evident, for example, by the titles of *The Unnamable* and the later 'dramaticule' *Not I*).

## Themes and ideas

The key theme to the play, which Beckett originally titled just *En attendant* (*Waiting*) (McMillan and Fehsenfeld 1988, 59), is of course the enduring, unending wait for salvation, clarification or purpose. This theme has been discussed above, as it is the central pillar of the play's narrative structure. The enigma of Godot, though, opens up a series of enquiries that permit us to consider other themes. There can be no denying that the name Godot might suggest to an audience that the figure the two tramps are waiting for is God, with the consequent possibility of a metaphoric suggestion that they are waiting for death, for the summation of their lives, for finally atrophied identities. Beckett once stated that 'if by Godot I had meant God I would [have] said God, and not Godot' (Knowlson 1997, 412), but he must have known that the choice of name permitted or even encouraged this interpretation. In adding the final '-ot' to the name, however, he also very clearly detracts from that possibility. The suffix also trivializes God; to a French ear, the '-ot' creates a diminutive form, as the suffix is commonly added to a proper name to create an affectionate term of address for a child or a pet. It was also commonly employed by clowns when inventing audience-friendly names, and the sweet Pierrot caricature is an obvious antecedent of the trend. Charlie Chaplin was held in such popular esteem by the French that he was (and still is) commonly spoken of as 'Charlot'. Adding the suffix '-ot' to 'God', then, is dismissive of that revered syllable, and therefore both a subtle, sly blasphemous act and a way of disconcerting the too easy interpretation of reading 'Godot' simply as 'God'. Beckett was happy to put people off the scent too, perhaps mischievously. He once explained to Roger Blin that the name was inspired by the French slang for boot ('godasse') (Bair 1990, 405) and on another occasion made reference to Tour de France spectators he met waiting for the cyclist Godeau to pass (Duckworth 1966, 1). Such deliberate red herrings effectively warn us that seeking fixed, single-answer interpretations is a fool's game.

Nonetheless, *Waiting for Godot* is saturated with Christian imagery and references to the Bible and these often serve thematic purposes. Within the first minutes of the play, Vladimir fails properly to recall Proverbs 33:12 ('Hope deferred maketh the heart sick but a desire fulfilled is a tree of life') and thereby initiates a few thematic strands – forgetfulness and failing memory, waiting (hope deferred) and some former dignity which these two figures might once have held (testified by such educated quoting, albeit faulty). The conversation soon after brings up mention of the four Gospels' inconsistency as regards the two thieves who were crucified alongside Christ, and while Vladimir is dismissive of the historical emphasis on the only version that mentions one of the thieves being saved, he is attracted to the odds of 50:50 that separate 'hope deferred' from 'desire fulfilled'. He of course conveniently overlooks the one in four odds (the Evangelists' memories of the incident) that diminish that hopeful chance. In his own situation, waiting for whatever salvation Godot might represent, he clutches at whatever straws make themselves available. Looming throughout the play, though, is a doom-laden sense that their waiting will be fruitless, and the two remain sick at heart to the end.

Their proposal that they might hang themselves from the lone onstage tree makes something of a potential cross of that single vertical aspect of scenery. Imagery of the cross and crucifixion is embedded elsewhere in the play, as when Vladimir and Estragon hold Lucky upright, his arms outstretched across their shoulders. Beckett emphasized this in his own *mise en scène* and, for example, had Pozzo fall across Lucky to form a cross shape, and asked Vladimir and Estragon to pace up and down and across the stage to describe, by their path, the shape of the cross (Knowlson 1993, 158, 161, 165–6).

There are references to Cain and Abel, the first sons of Adam and Eve. When Pozzo calls for help, having entered blind and fallen down in the second act, in order to determine his identity Estragon calls out names, beginning with Abel. He assumes that Pozzo's cry in response is confirmation of the name and calls Lucky Cain, only for Pozzo to cry out once more and Estragon to declare that 'He's all humanity' (83). This indicates the function of characters as representing all of human endeavour that Beckett perhaps intended. Vladimir earlier stated that 'all mankind is us' when, in the second act, Pozzo falls and cries for the two tramps' help, embracing his function as a representative of his race: 'Let us represent worthily for once the foul brood to which cruel fate consigned us!' (79). In the first act, when Estragon responds to Pozzo's request to know his name, he responds 'Adam' (37), again perhaps identifying himself as representing all mankind. The boy who comes at the end of each act speaks of having a brother and, like Abel, tends livestock. His brother, like Cain, is punished. In Genesis, Cain is cursed to wander the earth by God for having killed his brother, and it is tempting to see a thematic attraction to Beckett in that fate.

That the boy speaks of tending goats while his brother tends sheep is reminiscent of Jesus' parable of the sheep and goats (Mt. 25:31–46) in which the sheep are blessed and the goats cursed. Here again, as with the two thieves and Cain and Abel, there is a pairing of distinct fates, a pairing which is captured in the quarrelling friends, in the passers-by Pozzo and Lucky, and which is symbolically attached to the two messenger boys. That Beckett has the shepherd punished, and not the goatherd, inverting the chastisement within the parable, both reinforces and subverts the 50:50 odds of security that Vladimir holds on to, while suggesting the random, and not morally-driven, infliction of suffering. The parable of the sheep and goats is commonly interpreted as relating to the day of judgement, when both the living and the dead will be judged as either worthy of eternal life in the kingdom of God or destroyed in eternal fire. Vladimir's reaction to hearing that Godot sports a white beard, typical of persistent Western iconography of the deity, is to appeal immediately to Christ for mercy; a fearful response that implies some association between judgement and his ever-deferred appointment with Godot. Indeed, all the references to the Gospels that the play invokes are concerned with issues of judgement, salvation and damnation, and Estragon's casual blasphemy of comparing himself with Christ (52) makes utter sense in this context.

Another key theme in the play is that of being seen, of being observed. On both occasions when the boy brings his message from Godot, Vladimir sends him back with the message that the boy has seen him and his friend. In both cases, he is concerned to impress the urgency of this upon the boy: 'You did see us, didn't you?' (52), 'You're sure you saw me' (92). To be observed, and have it confirmed that one has been seen is, at the most basic level, a confirmation that one exists, that one participates and matters in the world. Observation is one step short of validation, the confirmation of self-worth. Whatever salvation or promise Godot represents for Vladimir and Estragon, they take a scrap of comfort in the thought that confirmation of their being seen might be conveyed. In a later work, *Film*, which is primarily concerned with observation of and by the self, Beckett employed philosopher Bishop Berkeley's phrase *Esse est percipi* (to be is to be perceived). Theologically applied, this statement clarifies that matter exists when no-one is there to perceive it because God sees all and therefore sustains all. Perhaps hinting at this, Estragon asks 'Do you think God sees me?' (76) and just prior to the boy's second act entrance, with Estragon asleep, Vladimir reflects 'At me too someone is looking' (91), comforting himself perhaps with the thought that God observes him, but also offering a clear metatheatrical nod to the audience who, in this case, replace God and sustain the actors' very *raison d'être*. Vladimir continues: 'of me too someone is saying, he is sleeping, he knows nothing, let him sleep on'. Is he referring to God here as a distant observer who leaves him to continue in his ignorance, or to the audience, who might themselves have come to this judgement of his and Estragon's characters by the end of the play? In this way, the metatheatricality of the play serves a thematic purpose in itself, and is articulate of what the play has to communicate.

Such metatheatricality is embedded within the text and at times becomes overt for comic purposes. Estragon, sarcastically admiring the 'charming spot', turns to the audience and states 'Inspiring prospects' (13–14). When Vladimir departs hastily to empty his bladder, Estragon indicates the location of the loos: 'End of the corridor, on the left' to which Vladimir responds 'Keep my seat' (35). The play is littered with such winks to the stalls: Estragon's phrase '[n]othing happens, nobody comes, nobody goes, it's awful' (41) is surely a tease, as is his 'I've been better entertained' (38) and Vladimir's tired 'And it's not over' (34). An indulgent, witty in-joke is added when the two men play a game of insulting one another, and the winning jibe is the loaded slur, uttered with relish, 'Crritic!' (75). In his 1978 revised text for a production in New York directed by Walter Asmus and based upon his own 1975 production, Beckett added to the metatheatrical jokes with a new line given to Vladimir: 'we're on a plateau, served up on a plateau' (Knowlson 1993, 158–9), punning the flat, plateau-like stage against the notion of being 'served up on a platter'. As well as indicating the sense that the characters are betrayed and vulnerable, such metatheatrical indications reference the audience (see also 'that bog' (15), and 'all these corpses' (64)) and thereby reinforce the theme of being observed.

The structural repetitions that form part of the play's architecture have been discussed above as examples of form expressing theme. Vladimir and Estragon have differing relationships with the various repetitions, it seems, and the function of memory in relation to these establishes a theme of remembering and forgetting. Vladimir, noticing the few leaves that have sprouted on the tree between acts, confidently declares that 'Things have changed since yesterday' (60), and manifests some signs of hope, which he attempts to impart to

Estragon by insistently pointing out the change. His friend, how-ever, rudely rebuffs this almost optimistic stance by insisting on the possibility of Godot not coming, and by focusing on the unchanging conditions of their existence. Memory of the past here participates in the construction of a hopeful future: Vladimir, of course, has to remember what the tree was like yesterday in order to notice that it has changed. This entirely ordinary and unremarkable fact is rendered remarkable in the play by Estragon's peculiar response: he fails to remember the previous existence of the tree or their thoughts of suicide by hanging themselves from it, has only an extremely vague memory of Pozzo and Lucky, and does not recog-nize the place where they are. His relationship with time is different to that of his friend, and he seemingly rejects the past as irrelevant once the experience has gone: 'I'm not a historian' (65) he dismiss-ively insists when asked to remember a point earlier in the same evening. Vladimir, on the other hand, engages in an almost nos-talgic attempt to evoke memories of other times and other places, pointing out the big difference between where they are now and 'the Macon country' where, he claims, they were employed as grape-pickers (62). In order to maintain hopes of future change, it is necessary to recall changes in the past. Estragon's persistent amne-sia, on the other hand, is perhaps a more truthful recognition of their condition. It may well be, as Estragon grumbles, 'never the same pus from one second to the next' (60), but that does not mean anything has actually changed:

> ESTRAGON: (*suddenly furious*). Recognize! What is there to recognize? All my lousy life I've crawled in the mud! And you talk to me about scenery! (*Looking wildly about him.*) Look at this muckheap! I've never stirred from it! (61)

Estragon is not unique in manifesting this persistent amnesia. Neither Pozzo nor the boy recognize or remember the two tramps, after all, and this unsettles us. As audience we are inclined to invest in Vladimir's memories as stable and inherently true, and believe that when Act II begins we are about to witness the next day in the lives of these odd people. Vladimir's assertions seem therefore reliable to us, but Beckett subverts such obedient audience 'reading' of stage narrative by piling the evidence against Vladimir as no-one else subscribes to his recollections. Even the rapid sprouting of leaves on a tree connives against Vladimir's stance and catches the audience out with a non-realistic device (the sudden leaves) which conspires against the realism of Didi's certainty that his act two day is the one that follows his act one experiences.

The tree's partial regeneration may well be, as critics have often noted, a sign of hope, but that hope is undermined. Seasonal cycles might bring change, but those changes are endlessly repeated from year to year. Spring will come around again and again, each time bringing hope, but each time also indicating the passage of time back to winter again. Time, then, brings some change, but does not alter the fundamental nature of the 'muckheap'. In fact, time tends to bring degeneration more than regeneration in *Waiting for Godot*. As Steven Connor has argued, there are two forms of repetition in the play: on the one hand there is the circular model which we have just outlined, but on the other is a linear model, whereby some of the repetitions that we perceive in the play 'seem to indicate not endless reduplication, but entropic decline' (Connor 1988, 121). The state of Pozzo and Lucky in Act II is the most obvious example of such decline: the once overbearing Pozzo is now blind, and Lucky, who in Act I had already degenerated to a state of inarticulacy, is now entirely dumb. Vladimir questions Pozzo about when this happened, eliciting the following enraged reply:

Have you not done tormenting me with your accursed time! It's abominable! When! When! One day, is that not enough for you, one day like any other day, one day he went dumb, one day

I went blind, one day we'll go deaf, one day we were born, one day we shall die, the same day, the same second, is that not enough for you? (*Calmer.*) They give birth astride of a grave, the light gleams an instant, then it's night once more. (89)

Decline, of course, leads to death, and indeed Vladimir himself has just observed that Pozzo is dying (83). Pozzo's vision of the brevity and futility of life is a key passage in the play, and is later echoed by Vladimir in another important passage:

Astride of a grave and a difficult birth. Down in the hole, linger-ingly, the grave-digger puts on the forceps. We have time to grow old. The air is full of our cries. (*He listens.*) But habit is a great deadener. (90–1)

The time passed waiting to grow old is thus a painful experience if we acknowledge the futile brevity of existence, but that pain might be 'deadened' by habit, or by various ways of making time seem to pass more quickly. Another provisional escape route is sleep, of course, and Estragon gets some brief respite from waiting in his occasional dozes, though even there he cannot fully escape suffering as he is tormented by nightmares. His friend refuses to listen to his accounts of them, perhaps not wanting to be drawn into his bleak imagination. Time passing, then, cannot be escaped, and Beckett demonstrates the human condition of being trapped in an insub-stantial present where purpose is elusive and has to be narrated, made up. The past is dredged up in the present to offer a sense of hope for the future, but the evidence of hollow repetitions indicates that all the future holds is more of the same.

## Close reading 1 – Lucky's 'think'

Lucky's speech (42–5) is both one of the most memorable parts of *Waiting for Godot* and one of the most confusing. The audience is just getting used to the inexplicable presence of these two new characters, when the miserable and subjugated Lucky, ordered by his master to 'think', spews out an apparently nonsensical pseudo-philosophical rant. For the characters on the stage, this speech is so shocking as to provoke violent physical attempts to make him stop; for the audience, it is one of the moments of the play that stays most vividly in our memories.

Beckett himself suggested that the speech held much greater and more subtle significance than we might at first assume. While directing the play in 1975, the author stated that it is in Lucky's speech that 'the threads and themes' of the play 'are being gathered together' (Graver 2004, 49–50). The monologue's theme was summarized by Beckett as 'to shrink on an impossible earth under an indifferent heaven' (Graver 2004, 50), and in his notebooks to the 1975 Schiller production, he divided the speech into three main parts: 'Indifferent heaven', 'Dwindling man' and 'Earth abode of stones' (Knowlson 1993, 291). This structure, according to Ackerley and Gontarski, recalls 'the music-hall demented lecture, with three incoherent premises, one major and two minor, but no logical reconciliation' (Ackerley and Gontarski 2006, 330). It also reflects the play's general concerns with the inscrutability of God (if he exists at all), the suffering of humanity, the futility of human 'progress' and the inevitability of death.

Everything about Lucky's tirade suggests uncertainty, ambiguity, and unknowability (apart, of course, from the one certainty of death and decay). Lucky has no more beliefs, and the monologue systematically undermines the efficacy of a number of ways of knowing, understanding or explaining the world ('grand narratives'), whether they be religious, scientific or philosophical. Under particular attack is Christianity: Lucky describes 'a personal God [...] with white beard' (42) who manifests 'apathia' (indifference to human suffering), 'athambia' (inability to be provoked into action) and 'aphasia' (loss of power to express or understand speech), who inexplicably fails to love some of us, and suffers for our sins 'for reasons unknown' (43). This terminal uncertainty is reflected in the repeated 'quaquaquaqua' with which Lucky punctuates his 'thinking'. According to Beckett, Lucky is trying here to say 'Quaquaquaquaversalis' (meaning 'a god who turns himself in all directions at the same time') (Knowlson 1993, 133), but his failure ends up instead echoing the French word 'quoi', meaning 'what', or the sound of a duck quacking.

All human research, inquiry, and interpretation – whether it be scientific, theological or philosophical – is dismissed in Lucky's 'think'. In the above theological context, for example, it is not merely God who is undermined, but also any attempt to use notions of divinity to explain human existence: the theologians who are credited with the above argument are named 'Puncher and Wattman', names which evoke violence (puncher) and uncertainty (what-man) as well as alluding to (and belittling) scientific progress (by reference to the Victorian inventor James Watt). Multilingual punning is also apparent here: their names derive from the original French 'Poinçon et Wattmann', with the comically mundane meanings 'ticket-puncher' and 'tram driver', and the implication that their progress is restricted to a given set of rails and a repeated routine. There are a number of named pairs of 'researchers' of various kinds in Lucky's tirade, all of whom are similarly undermined by comic naming: we also have the obscenely named 'Testew and Cunard' from the 'Acacacacademy of Anthropopopometry of Essy-in-Possy' ('Testew' and 'Cunard' pun on male and female genitalia; 'caca' and 'popo' are infantile French terms for 'poo' and 'potty'), and reference to the unfinished labours of 'Fartov and Belcher' (who need no introduction). The work of all the named researchers is explicitly 'unfinished' or is in some way inconclusive, and the most repeated phrase in relation to their work (and indeed throughout the passage) is, tellingly, 'for reasons unknown'. Lucky's key 'message' is that, in spite of theological questioning, scientific research, advances in medicine ('penicilline and succedanea' (43), the drug or any substitute) and healthy living ('alimentation', 'physical culture' and 'sport of all sorts'), man nonetheless 'is seen to waste and pine' and 'shrink and dwindle' (43–4). 'Progress' is merely an illusion, and, apart from the inevitable decline, nothing really changes.

These themes are all crucial, but Lucky's speech is, of course, particularly remarkable for its language, and especially for the extent to which it manages to make language appear arbitrary and ineffective (a feature of language in the play which we commented on above). Lucky switches abruptly and confusedly between different topics and different points, often mid-phrase and usually regardless of context or syntax. Academic language is parodied particularly effectively here: inconclusive reasoning is foregrounded through the repetition (with some variation) of phrases such as 'for reasons unknown but time will tell', 'the labours left unfinished', 'in the light of the labours lost of', and 'the labours abandoned left unfinished'. The form of the language itself mirrors such inconclusiveness: the 'speech' is unbroken by punctuation, and Lucky's last word before he is finally silenced is 'unfinished'. A proliferation of empty rhetorical phrases such as 'but who can doubt it', 'that is to say', 'beyond all doubt', 'but what is more', 'as a result of', 'it is established', 'in brief', 'in short', 'I resume', are used, apparently indiscriminately, to delay the progression of the sentence towards any conclusions, and indeed to make us forget even that anything was going to be 'established' in the first place.

The above literary analysis of Lucky's speech indicates how crammed it is with thematic referents. When listening to Lucky as audience, however, it is difficult even to discern that meaning is being deferred in the ways outlined. We simply do not have the time to consider the speech's content as it is frantically uttered, quickly and mechanically, and as our attention is partially drawn to the motions and responses of the three other characters. In performance, the speech functions through the rhythmic and phonetic aspects of language being foregrounded to such an extent that we perceive the sounds of words over and above their meanings. On the one hand, this is achieved through the frequent repetition of words and phrases. On the other hand, Beckett makes some very effective use of rhythmic patterning throughout the monologue. The rhythms of the speech as a whole are, like its meaning, broken up and inconsistent, but one particular refrain does keep recurring and can be perceived, for example, in the following phrases: 'for reasons unknown that as a result', 'for reasons unknown of Testew and Cunard', 'in view of the labours of Fartov and Belcher', 'in spite of the strides of physical culture', 'for reasons unknown no matter what matter', 'in the year of their lord six hundred and something', 'for reasons unknown in spite of the tennis' and 'in spite of the tennis the labours abandoned'. If we were analysing these phrases as lines of poetry, we would observe that they are all tetrameters, and that, although they are made up of a combination of iambic and anapaestic feet, they are predominantly in triple meter, creating a noticeable 1-2-3 rhythm. This rhythmic pattern comes up frequently in the monologue (the above phrases are only a few examples), and it makes the phrases stand out from the surrounding prose. In doing so, we have time as audience to latch on to the phrases which we make out in the blur of words, but as these phrases are about incapacity, failure or incompleteness, they only compound any frustration we might experience in the moment at trying to make out any discernable sense. The pattern also makes us focus on the rhythms of the adjacent phrases which break up or interrupt the strong forward motion of the triple meter, thus bringing our attention to rhythm more generally. What is more, triple meter is generally associated with comic verse, an association which would help undermine the seriousness of the arguments which Lucky is garbling, while also subtly contributing to the general humour of the scene: the words may sound like attempts at seriousness, but the delivery tells us it is to be laughed at.

## Close reading 2 – Leaves / sand / leaves

Vladimir and Estragon have just been reunited at the beginning of Act II, and have reconciled themselves to the fact that they do not seem to be able to leave each other, even though Vladimir makes Estragon miserable, and Estragon enrages Vladimir by refusing to remember most of what had happened the day before. Estragon suggests that Vladimir kill him, but in the absence of any such decisive action, or indeed of anything happening, Estragon suggests that they 'try and converse calmly, since we are incapable of keeping silent' (62). What follows is a dialogue which serves, thematically, to undermine language as a mode of expression or communication. But whereas Lucky's speech in Act I had been a violent and shocking assault upon language, here the dialogue is notable for its gentle lyricism. Language is being undermined in a very different way.

Thematically, the passage has much in common with the linguistic issues raised by the incomprehensibility of Lucky's speech. Lucky's language is terminally evasive and inconclusive; here, Vladimir and Estragon are 'incapable of keeping silent', but their words do not intend to define or describe the world any more than do Lucky's:

VLADIMIR:     You're right, we're inexhaustible.
ESTRAGON:   It's so we won't think.
VLADIMIR:     We have that excuse.
ESTRAGON:   It's so we won't hear.
VLADIMIR:     We have our reasons.

Their words, Estragon admits, are not supposed to *mean* anything. We have, by this point in the play, got used to Didi and Gogo's banter as being just another way of 'passing the time'. What this passage makes clear, however, is that their talk is even more insignificant than we might initially have thought: words are a way of covering up experience, and of preventing the talkers from having to confront the true nature of their condition. What follows is a lyrical interchange about what Estragon calls 'the dead voices':

| | |
|---|---|
| VLADIMIR: | They make a noise like wings. |
| ESTRAGON: | Like leaves. |
| VLADIMIR: | Like sand. |
| ESTRAGON: | Like leaves. |
| | *Silence* |
| VLADIMIR: | They all speak together. |
| ESTRAGON: | Each one to itself. |
| | *Silence* |
| VLADIMIR: | Rather they whisper. |
| ESTRAGON: | They rustle. |
| VLADIMIR: | They murmur. |
| ESTRAGON: | They rustle. |
| | *Silence* |
| VLADIMIR: | What do they say? |
| ESTRAGON: | They talk about their lives. |
| VLADIMIR: | To have lived is not enough for them. |
| ESTRAGON: | They have to talk about it. |
| VLADIMIR: | To be dead is not enough for them. |
| ESTRAGON: | It is not sufficient. |
| | *Silence* |
| VLADIMIR: | They make a noise like feathers. |
| ESTRAGON: | Like leaves. |
| VLADIMIR: | Like ashes. |
| ESTRAGON: | Like leaves. |
| | *Long Silence* |
| VLADIMIR: | Say something! |
| ESTRAGON: | I'm trying. |
| | *Long Silence* |
| VLADIMIR: | (*in anguish*). Say anything at all! |

There are a number of ways in which we can interpret what exactly the 'dead voices' are, but it is important also to allow for the text's ambiguity, and thus to remain open to different interpretations. On one level, we can read this literally: the 'dead voices' might allude to the voices of the dead. (Bearing in mind when the play was written, we might, for example, relate this to the dead and disappeared of World War Two, and the sense of loss and horror attached to their memories.) On another level, the 'voices' could be those of humanity in general, and thus also Vladimir and Estragon's own; the voices are 'dead' because language is 'dead'. Estragon has just described how compulsive and how arbitrary their own chatter is, and it seems that this experience is not exclusive to them. 'They' (whoever 'they' might be) cannot just live, 'They have to talk about it'. Vladimir's own anguished response to silence confirms both how necessary, and how indiscriminate, that talking is: 'Say anything at all!'

This passage is therefore extremely significant thematically. It is perhaps most notable, however, for its curiously 'poetic' qualities. For example, the five lines from 'It's so we won't think' to 'All the dead voices' are remarkably rhythmically regular for dramatic dialogue that is not explicitly in verse form: all five lines are of uniform length, and the first three are rhythmically identical (an iambic followed by an anapaestic foot). Indeed, this particular rhythm is alluded to later in the passage, in the line 'They all speak together' and in the lyrical sequence 'like feathers. / Like leaves. / Like ashes. / Like leaves.' Add to this the lilting rhythms of the sequence 'they whisper. / They rustle. / They murmur. / They rustle.' and we have language which, although not actually verse, constantly alludes to and skirts around the rhythms of poetry. Additional effects are created through a manipulation of the phonic qualities of words, many of which are also onomatopoeic, such as: 'whisper', 'rustle', 'murmur', 'feathers', 'ashes', 'leaves'. The actress Billie Whitelaw once commented on the 'dramatic rhythms of Beckett's word-music' (Whitelaw 1995, 78), and indeed, Beckett's language here begins to work on us in different ways: like music, such language affects us emotionally rather than signifying anything very clearly, thus leading us towards an experience of language rather than a rational 'understanding' of it.

But if this passage is supposed to undermine language, why does Beckett choose such beautiful language with which to do so? One response to this question is to consider how Beckett might be implicitly commenting on poetry and on poetic lyricism in general. Traditionally, in poetry, the sounds and rhythms of language are manipulated in order to make sound correspond to sense (ono-matopoeia being one of the most evident examples of this), or at least to make sound emphasize the meanings of words. In this passage, however, rhythmic and phonetic patterning tends instead to draw our attention to the sounds over and above the meanings of words (an effect which we also find in Lucky's speech, albeit mani-fest in a very different way). In this regard, the passage embodies its own thematic focus. It is about using language to obscure experi-ence and to prevent the speakers from having to face reality. Its own lyricism does just that: the beauty of the language contrasts with the despair that it is attempting to cover up – a despair and anguish which rises to the surface in the scripted silences. If talking is a compulsion to obscure the true nature of experience, then might not lyricism be merely a particularly effective example of this? If we take this interpretation on board, then the 'poetry' of this passage can be seen to be making an ironic comment on the superficiality of poetic 'beauty'. Perhaps here the modernist/postmodernist rift is most clearly visible; the modernist would embrace the beauty of the language, while a postmodernist temperament might emphasize its falseness.

Consider the effect of this lyricism on an audience. The gentle lilt of the rhythms, and short bursts of short phrases, spoken slowly, have a pleasing, calming effect. If, as is stated above, the passage demonstrates how language is used to obscure experience and to prevent the speakers from having to face reality, then it has a similar distracting effect on the audience. We are lulled by the gently paced delivery and we are attracted by the regularity of the rhythm. As such, we are not being encouraged to listen to what is spoken, to be concerned about who these dead voices might actually be, but simply invited to relax into the words. Once again, form supersedes content, and delivers theme by giving the audience an experience of what is being expressed, not clarifying it.

# 3 Production History

## World debut at the Théâtre Babylone, Paris. Directed by Roger Blin (1953)

*Waiting for Godot* was first performed in French at the Théâtre Babylone, Paris, in January 1953, and was directed by Roger Blin. The Babylone theatre offered a humble birth to this most significant of twentieth-century plays. The location was a converted refectory on the Boulevard Raspail, south of the Seine. Its stage measured only six metres wide by four deep, and the auditorium had a capacity of just 230. It was located away from the commercial theatre scene in Paris, and was run by theatre enthusiast Jean-Marie Serreau as a space for new playwrights and new theatre innovations.

Roger Blin was an actor with a significant reputation in such off-mainstream, avant-garde environments. He had been a close friend of Antonin Artaud, and had acted as his assistant director on the 1935 production of *Les Cenci* and featured in his *Pour en finir avec le jugement de Dieu* (*To Have Done with the Judgement of God*) in 1947. In the years prior to *Godot*, his reputation had been consolidated by his appearance as the devil in Henri Pichette's surreal verse play *Les Épiphanies* alongside the box-office stars Gérard Philipe and Maria Casarès. The critics welcomed his debut as a director at the Gaîté-Montparnasse theatre, where, in 1949, he mounted an Irish drama by one of Beckett's contemporaries, Denis Johnston, and August Strindberg's *Ghost Sonata*. He went on to direct his friend Arthur Adamov's first play, *La Parodie*, in 1952 while looking for a theatre to house Beckett's play.

In 1949, Beckett had sent his recently completed script of *Waiting for Godot* to numerous Paris theatre managers and it was rejected by each and every one. The author was beginning to despair of ever seeing his play performed and only his partner Suzanne had any enthusiasm left to keep pursuing new avenues of opportunity. Towards the end of the year, she took the script to Roger Blin at the Gaîté-Montparnasse and went with Beckett to see his production of Strindberg's play there. What Beckett saw must have impressed him, as he went to see the production a second time. Perhaps he was reassured by Blin's respectful treatment of Strindberg's text, or by the integrity and lack of commercial concerns that surrounded the production. The two men struck up a friendship, and Blin began what was to prove a three-year search for a theatre that would accept his production of the remarkable text he had received. Various possibilities came and were lost, and it was only upon receipt of a government subsidy for new writing that Blin was finally able in 1952 to convince Jean-Marie Serreau to open the Babylone theatre to Beckett's play.

Beckett sat in on many of the later rehearsals for this debut production. At first he was troubled by Blin's directing methods, which seemed to lack all methodology. Deirdre Bair recounts how Blin 'would come into the theatre ready to rehearse whatever lines interested him most at that particular moment' and writes of how he 'seemed to be distracted and vague, to drift off into mental reaches known only to himself' (Bair 1990, 423). At this point in his life, Beckett still had no practical experience of the rehearsal room, and implicitly trusted Blin, rarely interjecting into the proceedings with any comments. Blin's job was to make theatrical sense of Beckett's non-conventional script:

> [Beckett] had indicated the movements and the timings perfectly
> well in his text, but these indications were for the reader first and

foremost; once on the stage things are different; you have to take into account the unfathomable personality of the actor, material requirements, the expressive value of certain words [. . .] he graciously accepted my ideas, looking *a priori* for a stylisation, and approved the adjustment they demanded in the execution. He proved not to be against discoveries, but he insisted that they were totally, organically, justifiable. (Taylor-Batty 2007, 100–1)

Blin had been rehearsing the play on and off for months, even before there was any contract signed or any theatre to stage it. He had been attracted to the play's formal structure, and particularly by what he saw as its provocative nature. At first he emphasized the comedic qualities of the characters' interaction, recognizing the influence of vaudeville or classic screen comedy such as Laurel and Hardy and Buster Keaton, but eventually he began to appreciate the tragic condition that Beckett portrayed, and the extended, broken rehearsal period perhaps assisted in cultivating a *mise en scène* that accentuated the play's multifaceted nature:

The traps, red herrings, allusions, the marked domination of the grammatical breathing rhythm were all concerns during the three years of rehearsal. First the lure of the circus [. . .] later the lure of farce, the lure of sentimentality, particularly as regards Vladimir. [. . .] I know that there are different levels in Godot, but you can't attain the desired magic without concentrating first and foremost on the most directly human level. For each character, I started quite simply with their physical impairments, either real or imagined. (Taylor-Batty 2007, 97)

Blin considered Vladimir's prostate ailment – his need constantly to pee – and envisaged him as agitated and in perpetual motion, moving around the stage, crossing from wing to wing and using this motion as of a piece with his being on the lookout for the arrival of

Godot. In contrast, the constantly hungry and sleepy Estragon was envisaged as always wanting to sit and rest. In this way, the director created a permanent visual contrast between the two; one mobile and standing, the other inclined to stay put and seated. He had already sought a visible contrast in his casting of the two roles: Lucien Raimbourg (Vladimir), a music-hall comic actor, was short and slim, while Pierre Latour (Estragon) was tall and large-framed. In casting this way, Blin was influenced by the vagrant pair in John Steinbeck's *Of Mice and Men*, as he was attracted by the visual and emotional paradox of the smaller man comforting the taller and stronger. In directing Raimbourg and Latour, rehearsals involved physicalizing the relationship between the two characters in terms of motion, dictated by an understanding of how the two men expressed a love–hate bond.

> Those two tramps seemed to me to have to blended physically each to the other, because their relationship is like that of an old couple which operates with a simultaneous physical attraction and repulsion. They need each other, they can't be apart for long, but they can't stand each other either. When they're happy, let them come together, their hugging becomes analogous with the systole and diastole of the beating heart. The physical connection which takes place at moments like that is so strong that, in their embrace, the image of the two of them coming together as one being is created. (Taylor-Batty 2007, 102–3)

Blin had cast a stocky actor in the role of Pozzo, to make for an intimidating presence, but the actor deserted the production with less than a month to go, and Blin was obliged to take the role himself and pad out his meagre frame to approximate the same effect. Thin and lanky, he had been more suited to the role of Lucky, which he had already learned and rehearsed. On adopting Pozzo, he asked his friend Jean Martin, of similar build, to take the role. Martin was taken by Lucky's bizarre mode of speaking his one lengthy line and, consulting Beckett, he adopted a kind of physical equivalent to the broken speech pattern that involved him jerking and shaking as though abandoned to muscular spasms. Blin, at first unsure of the performance, was finally convinced by the effect when a friend responded to Lucky's speech in rehearsal by feeling physically sick.

As with Vladimir and Estragon, Blin chose to find a way of representing Pozzo through the character's physical presence. He played Pozzo as led by his fat stomach, out of breath and with flat feet splayed as he walked. By physicalizing the characters' presence and motion in these ways, Blin and his actors discovered their emotional lives, and how to express these, through gestural and choreographical means. This process enabled the play to be structured while avoiding the unnecessary distraction of needing to contemplate the intellectual issues the text might be deemed to address. Blin was certainly aware of and inspired by the thematic material of the text, but in the rehearsal room he sought a stylization grounded in the bare facts that could be gleaned from the text: that there are two men waiting for a third who fails to arrive, but who meet two others that represent both threat and opportunity; that time needs to be killed; that the two men cannot separate, but irritate one another.

Beckett had written no indications in his text that gave an idea of how the characters should appear, except that all four wear bowler hats, and that Estragon wears the 'rags' that he uses jokingly as evidence that he was once a poet. Given their itinerant status, seemingly lost in an unnamed, barren wilderness, it seemed straightforward to Blin to dress his protagonists as tramps, effectively replicating visually the ambiguity of their status and history that the text projects. Vladimir's use of language set him apart from the rest, so Blin gave Latour a stiff collar and tie to wear, and a long morning coat to suggest a more dignified past. Pozzo was dressed as a rich landowner, in riding boots and jodhpurs, pinned cravat and collar, and a watch and chain hanging from his waistcoat pockets. Jean Martin as Lucky was dressed to signify a French servant of the previous century, with a long red jacket with gold braiding and a striped sailor's vest. To add to the character's indignity, Blin gave Lucky a hint of the clown by having Martin wear trousers that were too short and shoes that were too big. Beneath his bowler hat, Martin had a wig of long white hair that would fall to his shoulders when the hat was removed.

There was very little budget to spare on set design, and this first incarnation of Beckett's play was presented in front of a makeshift but effective solution. A backcloth was constructed from off-cuts of material sewn together and hung to obscure the rear brick wall of the theatre. Blin himself designed and constructed the tree by wrapping crepe paper around a wire frame, which was then stuck into a block of foam rubber. Another such block was placed elsewhere to effect an undulating stage surface, and both served to hide the lanterns used to cast upward lighting onto the backcloth to give a crepuscular effect. The characters were then lit with stark lighting from the front and above. Lighting effects had to be cheap and simple, which in turn participated in the non-naturalistic stage visuals. For example, to represent the rapidly rising moon that Beckett's text denotes, Blin asked a stagehand to stand behind the backcloth and manually raise a lantern with its glare up against the cloth.

On the whole, the play was warmly received by the theatre critics. Marcel Frère, the critic of the left-wing journal *Combat* described the drama as 'a profoundly poetic work, a desperate work of an author animated by a great epic breath' (Frere 1953) while Jacques Lemarchand in *Figaro Littéraire* praised it as 'a profoundly original work' and astutely recognized that the play 'leads the way for a whole new dramatic movement which is still in discovery' (Lemarchand 1953). Praise also came from Beckett's peers. The experimental novelist Alain Robbe-Grillet, already an admirer of Beckett's prose, immediately understood the significance of Beckett's re-writing of the rules of theatrical engagement:

> We suddenly realize, as we look at them, the main function of theatre, which is to show what the fact of *being there* consists in. For this is what we have never seen on the stage before, or not with the same clarity, not with so few concessions and so much force. (Robbe-Grillet 1965, 113)

The celebrated playwright Jean Anouilh, one of the most respected names on the contemporary French theatre scene, compared the production to that of the 1923 Parisian première of Luigi Pirandello's *Six Characters in Search of an Author* – a play that had had a profound influence on French dramatic writing – and described Blin's production as a 'music-hall sketch of Pascal's *Pensées* as played by the Fratellini clowns' (Graver 2004, 92). The *Pensées* ('thoughts') of Blaise Pascal, a seventeenth-century French philosopher, were a series of commentaries on man's relationship with existence as clarified by the Christian faith. The Fratellini clowns, archetypes of modern clowning with their wigs and big noses, had done much to revive the popularity of the circus in France in the first three decades of the twentieth century, and were adored by the Parisian public. Anouilh's description would have made clear to contemporary French audiences exactly what to expect, stamped with his influential seal of approval.

## The first production in English. Arts Theatre, London. Directed by Peter Hall (1955)

News of the remarkable success of Beckett's play in Paris, and subsequently in Germany, found its way back to London arts circles. The producer and impresario Donald Albery took an option out on the play and originally hoped to employ Alec Guinness and Ralph Richardson as the first British Vladimir and Estragon couple. His intention was to mount a large, star-led, West End production, in contrast to the humble French origins of the play. Ralph Richardson even arranged to meet Beckett to ask a series of questions he had compiled about the curious script he had received through the post. Meeting the artist backstage in his dressing room at the Haymarket, the author simply apologized – 'I'm awfully sorry, but I can't answer any of your questions' (Cronin 1997, 438) – and the esteemed actor rejected the script for one he could better understand.

Beckett had agreed in 1953 to write an English translation of the play for this projected West End production and for a production in the United States. One of the difficulties the producer faced, in addition to failing to secure star names, involved the troubles the script was getting into on the censor's desk. British theatre at this time (and up until the law changed in 1968) had to answer to the Lord Chamberlain's office and all play scripts had to be submitted for his approval. Beckett was asked to adjust some lewd references ('Fartov' became the anodyne 'Popov' for example) but he refused to remove the references to erections or the falling of Estragon's trousers, and resisted the deletion of many passages deemed blasphemous (such as Lucky's first fifteen lines) which the censor required before the play might be performed in public. Albery eventually was able to circumnavigate some of these demands by arranging for the production to run at the private Arts Theatre Club, where audiences comprised subscribing members, thereby bypassing the legal requirements regarding 'public' performances. Though the production was better financed than the French première (for which neither Blin nor Beckett were paid), the stage space was not much bigger than that at the Babylone, and the audience capacity at the Arts offered only a hundred seats more.

The director whom Albery approached was the young Cambridge graduate Peter Hall, the new artistic director of the Arts Theatre.

Hall was in his mid-twenties, with a small but significant portfolio of directing classic and contemporary plays at Cambridge University, the Oxford Playhouse and in London. He was building something of a reputation for his interest in continental writing, and was one of the first to present the new avant-garde plays that were circulated from across the channel and the Atlantic at that time. He mounted Federico García Lorca's *Blood Wedding* and Eugène Ionesco's *The Lesson* at the Arts in the year before the Beckett play (the first Ionesco play to be seen on the British stage) and preceded the run of *Waiting for Godot* with Eugene O'Neill's *Mourning Becomes Electra*. Hall cast Peter Woodthorpe in his first professional stage appearance as Estragon, and two other unknown actors, Paul Daneman and Timothy Bateson as Vladimir and Lucky. Peter Bull, who played Pozzo, was the only actor with any reputation and, though he commanded a higher fee than his colleagues, he also made it known how much he disliked the play.

Peter Snow, the stage designer for the production, perhaps naively felt that Beckett's sparse indications of 'A country road. A tree' (7) needed some embellishment. His design was nevertheless attuned to the themes of decay and desolation in Beckett's play. The country road was depicted as being under construction, or more likely abandoned, with the raw materials and instruments discarded stage right: a tar barrel and a pile of cobble stones. The tree had a bulky, robust trunk and a few scrawny branches just stretching over the actors' heads. At its base, Snow added reeds, in consideration for the actors who he intuitively recognized would appreciate some comfort from a more cluttered environment rather than being straightforwardly exposed to an audience on a bare stage (Worth 1999, 28). The designer set his tree upstage left on a raised platform, from which descended a slope for the actors to walk up, and a steeper decline on the other side of the stage with raised areas on ground level where Estragon might sit. The set was capably lit to provide a sense of dusk, with the lighting from above and below of a backcloth being the key element in assuring this effect. Roger Blin's solution of creating the sudden rise of the moon by having a spotlight rise up above and close to the backcloth was replicated here.

Like Blin, Hall was attracted to the poetry of the text, identifying 'a voice, a rhythm, a shape that was very peculiar: lyrical, yet collo-quial; funny, yet mystical' (Hall 1993, 103). Unlike Blin, he had a short (more conventional) rehearsal period and, despite not having 'the foggiest idea what some of it means' (Knowlson 1997, 414), knew he had no time for pontificating and theorizing: 'I don't understand the play and we are not going to waste time trying to understand it' he told his actors (Knowlson and Knowlson 2006, 122). His attitude was that progress had to be made in the rehearsal room if the play was to have any shape on its first night.

He began by rehearsing the clowning he felt was inherent to the play, and much of the final performance contained passages played straightforwardly for laughs, as though to keep a confused audience on-side. For example, David Bradby points out how some of the lines were delivered 'in the manner of someone reciting a work by Edward Lear or Lewis Carroll' (Bradby 2001, 77–8), the actors clearly treating difficult text as though it were simply nonsense. To this was added large, comedic gestures and playful acting, amplify-ing the stage-image to appeal visually. The costume choices conspired somewhat in this comic tone. Pozzo wore gaiters, plus-fours, a cra-vat and a garish checked coat, constructing an English landowner stereotype that persists today in comedy sketches. Vladimir and Estragon wore shabby and dusty trousers and coats that emphasized their vagabond nature. Indeed, as rehearsals progressed Hall shifted the emphasis away from Vladimir and Estragon as clowns and con-sidered them straightforwardly as tramps. He even had Vladimir emerge at the beginning of the second act from the abandoned tar barrel, as if it had been his makeshift bed for the night. Lines that were considered ponderous or reflective, such as Vladimir's final monologue, were delivered with a slow, sonorous pathos that was perhaps guilty of trying to layer meaning onto the words. Hall even had occasion to reign the actors in once the production was up and running, insisting that they stop trying to clarify the text with emphases of these sorts in their acting, and recite it without dramatic embellishment (Bradby 2001, 79).

The play opened on 3 August 1955 at the Arts and transferred to the Criterion theatre in September, drawing audiences until the following May. Those who came to the first performances were bemused. The resolutely unimpressed Peter Bull recalled how '[w]aves of hostility came whirling over the footlights, and the mass exodus, which was to form such a feature of the run of the piece, started soon after the curtain had risen' (Knowlson 1997, 414). Early critical notices accused the production of pointlessness and pretentiousness. Typical of these, Milton Shuman in the *Evening Standard* dismissed the production as 'another one of those plays that tried to lift superficiality to significance through obscurity'. The company survived a first week of half-empty houses before the production's fortunes were reversed by the weekend reviews of influential critics Harold Hobson and Kenneth Tynan. Hobson in the *Sunday Times* urged audiences to see the production, promising that the experience would be 'something that will securely lodge in the corner of your mind for as long as you live' (Hobson 1955). Tynan (1955) in The *Observer* predicted that in years to come, it will be fashionable to claim to have been present at that first English production of *Waiting for Godot*, and such a claim was indeed to hold no small cachet in arts circles for decades.

Beckett himself eventually saw the production after its transfer to the Criterion where, it being a public theatre, he had to suffer some of the cuts and re-writes he had strongly resisted. He sat through the production beside Alan Schneider, the American director who was to mount a production in the United States. Schneider remembers Beckett cringing and whispering to him how things were just not right. He disliked the setting, which he had wanted sparse and empty, disapproved of Hall's decision to add music by Béla Bartók to the beginnings and ends of the acts and he referred to Vladimir's excessive ponderous speech at the end of the play as displaying too much 'Anglican fervour' (Knowlson 1997, 417). These and similar remarks aside, he was impressed with Hall's achievement in many ways, and was particularly impressed by Peter Woodthorpe's work.

## Peter Hall's revivals (1997 and 2005)

Peter Hall went on to have a distinguished career in the British theatre, including periods as director of the Royal Shakespeare Company (which he founded in 1960) and of the National Theatre (from 1973 to 1988). He was knighted for his services to the arts in 1977. He was to return to Beckett's play twice. The first occasion was in 1997, at the Old Vic theatre where his Peter Hall Company was based. He later revived the play once more to celebrate the fiftieth anniversary of his first production, mounting it in 2005 during a summer residency at the Theatre Royal, Bath.

The director first returned to the play in 1997 with the ambition of correcting his youthful approach to the work, and doing justice finally to a text that he felt had done a good deal to instruct him in the theatre and which had so healthily bolstered his early reputation. In approaching the play afresh, Hall made use of the heavily edited and annotated text of the play that James Knowlson had compiled based on the rehearsal notes from Beckett's own production of the play (see pp. 66–73). He chose not to employ the movements and choreography inscribed in that edition, however, preferring to permit himself and the actors to discover their own *mise en scène* in the rehearsal room. The play by then of course had become a classic of the world repertoire, and attracting accomplished actors was no longer an issue. Vladimir and Estragon were played by Alan Howard and Ben Kingsley respectively, both unseen on the British stage at that point for over a decade. Denis Quilley played Pozzo and Lucky was performed by Greg Hicks.

While the 1955 production had been stylized, with an almost expressionistic set and deliberate comic flourishes, the 1997 production tended towards a sparser mode of representation which was more realistic in its detail. The set was stripped to the bare essentials of a scrawny tree, thin as a pole, its two branches barely lifting themselves over the actors' heads. This sprouted upstage left from an undisguised stage floor of traditional oak boards. Only Estragon's seat of a rock, downstage right, broke this flat surface. In this environment, Vladimir and Estragon were presented as simultaneously actors and characters, exposed to the glare of the audience with only the ominous, dimly lit wings of indeterminate depth either side of them.

The characters spoke in an Irish accent, in accord with the distinctive Irish dialectic lilt of the English text. The costumes were straightforwardly realistic, and the two key protagonists were dressed as shabby, unwashed vagrants. Controversially perhaps, Beckett's bowler hats were replaced in this production: Estragon wore a reversed flat cap, Vladimir a weather-beaten trilby and Lucky had a ridiculous-looking, battered stovepipe hat. The relationship between the four men as an interlocked theatrical representation of mankind was weakened by the loss of this unifying element, but a noteworthy benefit was gained. As the play draws to a close, Vladimir is wearing Lucky's hat which, as the audience has seen, had extraordinary qualities in drawing forth Lucky's speech when placed upon its bearer's head in the first act. Where bowler hats are used, the fact that Vladimir ends up wearing Lucky's hat after the comic exchange of headgear in the second act is something that could be forgotten by the viewer of a performance. In choosing this realistic variation of hat choices, Hall effected the image of Vladimir's philosophizing monologue being spoken while conspicuously wearing Lucky's tall hat. Given what we have seen of Lucky's fate, this had the effect of validating the speech as thoughtful and heartfelt on the one hand and diminishing the value of Vladimir's intellectual endeavour on the other. As such, the hat acted as a visual footnote, an icon of both the comedic and the pathetic that underlined the two tramps' waiting game as they sat to offer their final lines on leaving but not leaving.

The relative realism of the production encouraged committed, invested performances from all four actors. The distinction between Vladimir and Estragon was extremely well contoured as a result, with Vladimir the undermined intellectual and Estragon the appalled, infuriated and reluctant time-passer, with always a cynical or dismissive turn of phrase with which to deflate his friend. The brutality of Pozzo and the savage bitterness of Lucky were also clearly portrayed. Bradby neatly compiles responses to the play that suggest that one result of this naturalism was that the crucial bond between Vladimir and Estragon was weakened, rendering their interdependence less convincing (Bradby 2001, 184). To a certain degree, too, when this classic of the theatre was performed by a cast of highly esteemed actors, it inevitably became something of a frame for virtuoso performances, however sensitively played. One result of this reverence, for example, was that Lucky's speech would be met each night by a round of applause.

Peter Hall's fiftieth anniversary production of *Waiting for Godot* was very much a revival of the 1997 *mise en scène*, though with a fresh cast of James Laurenson (Vladimir), Alan Dobie (Estragon), Terence Rigby (Pozzo) and Richard Dormer (Lucky). The production opened at the Theatre Royal, Bath, in September 2005. It transferred to the New Ambassadors theatre in London thirteen months later, after an unfortunate and unhappy quarrel with the Barbican. The Barbican had been unable to offer Hall a slot for his production within the anniversary year as they were hosting a rival anniversary production, directed by Walter Asmus. For this 2005 production, the same bare boards bore the actors, and the tree (with a more stout but no less scrawny trunk) and rock still provided the only stage elements. A significant visual difference here was the age of the tramps, with both Vladimir and Estragon sporting unkempt, grey beards, played by actors in their sixties and seventies. Detracting from the vaudeville of the original, and if anything adding to a gritty realism that Hall had captured in the 1997 production, the representation of the tramps as closer the end of their life than the beginning, and still waiting for whatever comfort or validation their mysterious rendezvous might provide, contributed to a more pathos-laden production. Seeing the play upon its transfer to the New Ambassadors, Michael Billington remarked upon Hall's work as 'a realistic elegy for the meaningless brevity of life' (Billington 2006).

## Samuel Beckett's own production at the Schiller-Theater, Berlin (1975)

In 1975, Samuel Beckett agreed to direct *Waiting for Godot*, in German (*Warten auf Godot*), at the Schiller-Theater in Berlin. His relationship with that theatre had been established a decade earlier when he agreed to assist in preparations for a production of the same play directed by Deryk Mendel. He later agreed to take on his first professional directing role there for a production of his *Endgame* (*Endspiel*) in 1967. He directed a production of *Krapp's Last Tape* (*Das letzte Band*) there in 1969, and then one of *Happy Days* (*Glückliche Tage*) in 1971. In agreeing to take on the directing responsibilities for his first and most famous play in 1975, he was effectively therefore completing a full set of *mises en scène* of all his longer plays, and perhaps satisfying himself that his vision of these plays could be fully revised and fine-tuned during the rehearsal processes for each.

Beckett began his preparations for his production of *Waiting for Godot* by re-acquainting himself with the original German language translation of his play. This text was the Suhrkamp Verlag edition (published in 1960) which had been produced by the translator Elmar Tophoven in 1953, following the Paris success of Roger Blin's production. Tophoven had consulted with Beckett closely over the translation and the edition had met with the author's approval. Returning to that text, Beckett expanded the stage directions or made some more precise, cut some dialogue and revised a good deal of it. He then put together his directing notebooks in which, page by page, he prepared his *mise en scène* ahead of rehearsals. He then updated these notes as the rehearsals were underway. The detailed notebooks and adjustments to the text were all compiled by James Knowlson and published in usefully annotated form in 1993, and these might be read as a new creative annexe to the play, as both Beckett's commentary upon it and also as a project of re-fashioning the text in line with the kinds of dramatic writing he had been engaged with since that first success.

Beckett was once asked if he saw anything new in his works when he returned to them to translate them. He answered: 'Yes. Mistakes' (McMillan and Fehsenfeld 1988, 182). The flippant humour of this remark is nonetheless evident in the attention to detail he committed to his notebooks for Schiller-Theater *Godot*, for which he noted that his desire was 'to give form to the confusion' (McMillan and Fehsenfeld 1988, 88). In this way, his interaction with the original text would result in changes being made to the previously published English text. For example, Beckett had never been fully satisfied with his English rendering of Estragon's original French verbal shrug each time he is reminded that he and Vladimir are waiting for Godot – 'C'est vrai'. The 'Ach ja' solution in the German translation was later applied to subsequent English versions, replacing the inadequate 'Ah' with a more despairing (and potentially sarcastic or cynical) 'Ah yes'. The textual changes to the German text were used to inform subsequent English productions directed by the assistant in Berlin, Walter Asmus, and as such, the revised English text that resulted is commonly considered now to be the definitive version of the play. It is this version of the text, for example, that Peter Hall was to employ for his 1997 and 2005 revivals.

The set and costume design for the production were provided by Matias Henrioud, who went by the professional name of simply Matias. Beckett had met him through Roger Blin when Matias designed the French première of Beckett's *Happy Days* in 1963 and subsequently employed him on all his work with the Schiller-Theater. The designer was a skilled visual artist, and was recognized for his ability to construct painterly atmosphere and location in his designs, rather than offer architectural contexts for actors. As such, he was perfectly suited to Beckett's theatre, which often was inspired by visual imagery. The stage set for the 1975 *Godot* was simple and economic. A pale bare tree – so slim that one might easily wrap one's hand around the trunk and touch thumb to fingers – stood upstage right, and had two meagre branches splayed at a 'v' from its trunk, one of which sprouted a pathetic twig at its extreme point. A rock was placed downstage right for Estragon. Between the two was an expanse of gently inclining stage floor placed upon and concealing the flat stage boards, creating a 'platter' upon which the actors would be served up. Efficient and sparse, the design visually foregrounded the actors in this frail space, effectively offering a background canvas upon which they would be the key scenic elements, and in which their gravitation towards and away from the stone and tree would be as articulate visually as anything they might utter. Beckett made this plain in his expressed vision of the visual contrast between his two main characters: 'Estragon is on the ground, he belongs to the stone. Vladimir is light, he is oriented towards the sky. He belongs to the tree' (McMillan and Fehsenfeld 1988, 140).

The cast of Beckett's production comprised Horst Bollmann and Stefan Wigger as Estragon and Vladimir, Carol Raddatz as Pozzo and Klaus Herm as Lucky. Bollman had been directed before by Beckett as Clov in *Endgame* at the Schiller-Theater and, with

Wigger, had played the same tramp couple in the 1965 production directed by Mendel. This group came together immediately in the rehearsal room, as Beckett chose to kick off his Berlin rehearsals by working on Lucky's speech, or 'think' as he called it. David Bradby (2001, 112) points out that this decision is the opposite of traditional rehearsal sequencing for the play, with the section often worked on late in the process, and he relates this decision to Beckett's recent experience in directing his contemporaneous writing of monologue texts *Not I* and *Footfalls*. Perhaps in this way Beckett sought to establish this section of the play as something of a keystone to the production, a kernel of the play's whole expression. By embedding it early into all four principal actors' minds it might serve to inform all subsequent work and discussion. Beckett broke the speech up into parts to facilitate rehearsal, and to indicate to the actor the elements of the fragmented argument that Lucky was pursuing. He rehearsed Pozzo, Vladimir and Estragon's responses of protestation and despair at the unending tirade, having the two tramps even seek (but fail) to escape the stage space. Crucially, Beckett explained that for Lucky the speech makes straightforward sense, but that he is frustrated by his inability to express as beautifully as he once could, telling the actor that Lucky 'would like to amuse Pozzo [. . .] Lucky would like to be successful' (McMillan and Fehsenfeld 1988, 139).

Contrary to his original textual indication, Beckett had Vladimir onstage at the beginning of both acts. In doing so, he suggested that neither of the tramps could escape the stage, that they are captives in their own drama, 'served up on a plateau' (Knowlson 1993, 158–9). He placed Vladimir upstage left, standing by the tree in half shadow at the play's opening. Estragon was sitting on a stone that Beckett had downstage right, thus establishing a visual relationship between the two men that also tied them to their tree/stone stations. (Though the original English text gives Estragon a mound, the original French and the German texts detail a stone.) Added to this visual connection, Beckett had Vladimir inspect his hat as

Estragon fiddled with his boots, establishing with this comedic image a binary between the two men: Estragon with his attachment to his physicality and bodily comfort, Vladimir with the cerebral and philosophical. In this way, as director, he sought to establish certain thematic strands of his play through gesture, motion and physical relationships, and to embed them early on in the stage action. These were often embellished presentations of his textual suggestions. So, for example, he wanted to emphasize the two tramps' sense of captivity by what he referred to in note-form as 'General effect of moves, especially V[ladimir]'s though apparently motivated [in fact] that of those in a cage' (Knowlson 1993, 98). The ambition was to develop a behavioural choreography that would become recognizable as the production progressed, and which sustained the notion that Estragon and Vladimir could not separate from one another. Beckett sought to capture this interdependency between the two key characters in Matias's design of their costumes. In the first act, Estragon and Vladimir had their own coats but Estragon wore Vladimir's dark trousers, which were too big for him, and Vladimir wore his companion's light striped trousers, which revealed his shins. In the second act, the costumes were swapped, so that each had trousers that were fine, but the jackets now were ill-fitting.

The bond between the two men was also visualized in a motif that Beckett wove throughout the play. This he referred to as 'approach by stages' in his notebook (Knowlson 1993, 400) and it was used as a recurring pattern of movement that established the 'perpetual separation and reunion' of Vladimir and Estragon. Examples of this 'approach by stages' are found in the 1993 revised text. Compare this passage with the same passage on page 15 of the original published text:

ESTRAGON:   (*Very insidious*) But what Saturday? And is it
Saturday? (*Advances towards Vladimir.*) Is it not

| | rather Sunday? (*Pause. Advances further.*) Or Monday? (*Pause. Advances further.*) Or Friday? |
| VLADIMIR: | (*Looking around him, as though the date was inscribed in the landscape*) It's not possible! |
| ESTRAGON: | Or Thursday? |
| VLADIMIR: | What'll we do? |
| ESTRAGON: | (*He returns to his stone.*) If he came here yesterday and we weren't here you may be sure he won't come again today. (*Sits.*) (Knowlson 1993, 14) |

The revision of the original text – with these indicators of Estragon's movements towards and away from Vladimir added to the original text – captures the repeating alternation in proximity between the two tramps in Beckett's production. With such details, he was able as director visually to effect the oscillations of attraction and repulsion between the two characters, like two magnets with switching poles, as well as a survival relationship which he referred to as symbiosis: 'It's all symbiosis' he once told Peter Woodthorpe, the first English Estragon, in response to a straightforward question as to what the play was about (Knowlson 1997, 417).

As with this 'approach by stages', Beckett sought to create very detailed, structured patterns within his *mise en scène* which would offer visual or rhythmic notes that emphasized the themes of his play. He wanted to emphasize the various repetitions embedded in the text that amounted to his protagonists being trapped in routine. Between the two acts of the play he effected numerous visual symmetries, where actions were repeated, but with contrasting variations. So, for example, Vladimir stands to Estragon's right when offering a carrot in Act I, but to his left when offering a radish in Act II; Pozzo and Lucky enter from stage right in Act I and stage left in Act II; Vladimir peers out with his hand screening his eyes into the right wings at the beginning of Act I, and the left wings in Act II; Vladimir's face indicates the pleasure of recognition when smelling Estragon's boot in Act II, whereas he had indicated disgust when doing so in Act I. Beckett also sought to demonstrate a slow ebbing and reduction within repetitions, to emphasize the wearing-down effect that routine has on the protagonists. Vladimir's inspections of his hat, for example, are thorough at first but later become only cursory. The repetition of the 'Let's go/We can't/Why not?/We're waiting for Godot' refrain was also something Beckett sought carefully to augment on each of its utterances, with the increasing desperation leading to the final abortive attempt at suicide. Another piece of stage business that participated in the detailed attention to repetitions was the manner in which the two tramps approached the tree, most notably on the two occasions where they contemplated hanging themselves from it. On all such occasions, Beckett would have Vladimir stand stage left of the tree and Estragon stage right, at such a distance from one another so as to frame the tree, creating a visual tableau that provided 'striking evocations of crucifixion imagery' (Knowlson 1993, 418).

Another motif that Beckett sought to establish was an emphasis on waiting, through the placement of what he referred to as 'Wartestellen' (waiting points) (Knowlson 1993, 418). Bradby describes these as 'fixed points of waiting, where everything stands completely still, where silence threatens to swallow everything up' before the action recommences (Bradby 2001, 116). Beckett decided to insert twelve such static moments in his play, creating what Knowlson refers to as 'brief but unmistakable tableaux' (Knowlson 1997, 91). He placed four at the beginnings and ends of each act and, with fastidious adherence to symmetry, four within each act. In this way, he constructed a scaffold of such moments that framed the action and gave his production a formal structure with the segments of action in compartments between these static moments of desperate waiting.

It is tempting to speak of this production as the definitive performance, but it is by no means certain that a production of a play directed by its author is the best version that can be arrived at. What is notable, though, is that in engaging practically with his play, Beckett was leaving behind an extended and meticulous commentary on that text. Though he would refuse to enter into such discussion verbally or in writing, by considering his choices in editing, translating and embellishing his text, and those he made in getting it to operate with actors on stage, we are left with a significant body of observations and interpretations made by the author that offer us a better understanding of his artistic objectives.

## Political Godot. Productions in Sarajevo (1993) and Haifa, Israel (1984)

When we go to the theatre and discover a production that has either pleasantly surprised or disappointed us by straying from what we know or expect of a familiar text, we speak of the director having applied his or her 'interpretation' and relate that – and in doing so perhaps form a judgement of value or worth – to what we consider to have been the author's intentions. Samuel Beckett's protectiveness of his own work for the stage was notorious and would lead on occasions to legal action to bar specific performances where a director's interpretation strayed, in his eyes, too far. Since his death the Beckett Estate has continued such action and, for example, Deborah Warner's 1994 London production of *Footfalls* deviated so far from the author's stage directions that the Estate intervened, insisted on certain changes, stopped a European tour of the production and placed a temporary embargo on Warner directing any other piece of Beckett's. While such extreme acts of protective censorship are rare, many productions of Beckett plays incite similar controversy, on diverse grounds. A French production of *Waiting for Godot* directed by Joël Jouanneau in 1990 had its stage constructed to represent a disused factory or warehouse, with Beckett's tree replaced by the shell of what looked like decrepit electrical apparatus (upon which three small green lights were lit in the second act). The production raised questions about the extent to which one can manipulate an author's work by imposing extraneous images and implying relationships and situations alien to the original material. Joanneau's rendering of the play involved the application of what Patrice Pavis (1992, 36–8) refers to as an ideotextual *mise en scène*, that is, one which attempts a dialogue between the text and the social conditions of its reception, in order perhaps to offer comment upon those conditions. In this way, for example, the director Shoji Koukami could justify an all-female production of *Waiting for Godot* in Japan by stating that culturally 'women are used to waiting while men are used to having women wait' making it therefore 'natural that women wait for Godot' (Oppenheim 1995, 42). An all-female production of the play at De Haarlemse Toneelschuur theatre in The Netherlands, however, had an injunction taken out against it by Beckett in 1988, though he failed to halt the run. To what degree does an 'ideotextual' *mise en scène* pervert the intentions of the playwright? Similar examples of this mode of approach applied to *Waiting for Godot* are the productions directed by Ilan Ronen and presented at the Haifa Municipal Theatre, Israel, in 1984 and directed by Susan Sontag in war-torn Sarajevo in 1993.

The version of *Waiting for Godot* performed at the Haifa Municipal Theatre, Israel, in November 1984 is of interest for its deliberate deviations from Beckett's text and for the significant local controversy it aroused, going as far as provoking calls in the Knesset – the Israeli parliament – for the production to be censored on the grounds of its 'subversive' content, and for the theatre's public subsidy to be revoked. The production was the second (after Athol Fugard's *The Island*) in a series of shows that were performed by the theatre in Arabic on a newly built 'Arabic stage'. Ronen employed two Arab actors, Yussef Abu-Varda and Muhram Khoury, to play Vladimir and Estragon respectively, and two Jewish actors to play Pozzo and Lucky: Ilan Toren and Dorn Tabori. A local Arab boy played Godot's messenger. It was this ethically specific casting and the ramifications this had on the reception of the text that was at the centre of all the controversy. In the words of one critic, the play became 'a parable about the ambiguous bonds which hold Jews and Arabs together' (Rapp 1985).

Vladimir and Estragon were presented as Palestinian labourers, dressed in overalls that were acutely resonant of the irony of Palestinians employed to work building Jewish settlements on land annexed by Israel from neighbouring Arab states. These two workers spoke in Arabic, with Estragon employing a more rural vernacular to Vladimir's more urbane vocabulary. Lucky spoke Arabic in a different accent to the two labourers. Some of the exchanges with Pozzo and Lucky took place in Hebrew. In a second version of the production, for Jewish audiences, the actors playing Vladimir and Estragon spoke Hebrew with distinct Arabic accents. Beckett's solitary tree was replaced by a perpendicular column of the sort of bulky construction wire used to reinforce concrete structures, partially filled with concrete at its base, leaving a skeletal scaffold frame reaching upwards. Concrete blocks were strewn on the stage floor, which was covered with sand and gravel, adding to the impression of an abandoned or suspended building site.

The director was unapologetic about his decision to use Beckett's text to articulate a situation that it had not been written to address: 'the play lent itself beautifully to the political treatment, as if it were intrinsic to it', he claimed (Oppenheim 1994, 244). Audiences concurred, though the responses of Jewish spectators differed in the main from those of Arabic spectators, with the latter split between Israeli and Palestinian Arab groupings. In response to the survey question 'To what extent has the performance succeeded in creating a local political possible world?', Arabic spectators responded by relating Godot to Palestine Liberation Organization leader Yasser Arafat, or to the promises of intervention or aid from neighbouring

Arabic countries, whereas Jewish audiences in general favoured an existential, universally applicable interpretation of the waiting in the play. Arabic spectators drew more specific social and political connotations for the play and, for example, made distinctions between Israeli Arab and Palestinian Arab in distinguishing the possible ethnicities of Vladimir, Estragon and Lucky in ways that Jewish spectators generally overlooked. The view of Pozzo drew markedly different responses, with 22 per cent of Jewish spectators opting to consider the character as 'anyone', while only 2 per cent of Israeli Arabs and 5 per cent of Palestinian Arabs concurred with this view, the majority opting instead to identify him as an 'exploiter' or 'oppressor'.[1]

A perhaps more extreme example of the play being adapted to purpose and situation is the production mounted at the Youth Theatre in war-torn Sarajevo in August 1993 by Susan Sontag. As a writer and cultural commentator, Sontag was no stranger to activism and controversy, and considered her decision to direct the play in a city under siege an act of solidarity with the beleaguered citizens of that city. The siege of Sarajevo lasted between 1992 and 1996 and was a central episode in the Bosnian War that erupted after the breaking up of the Socialist Republic of Yugoslavia in 1991. The war was fought between the army of the newly declared independent state of Bosnia and Herzegovina and the Bosnian Serb forces who fought for the creation of a Serbian republic and to maintain a form of Yugoslav federation. Sarajevo, as the administrative capital of the territory, was heavily fought over. Bosnian Serb forces blockaded the city early in the conflict, and maintained a stranglehold over it for nearly four years. An estimated 12,000 people died in the city during the siege, the most protracted in modern European history.

Sontag felt compelled to make a humanist gesture in support of the besieged citizens of Sarajevo, and arranged to enter the city to direct a stage play that might speak to their plight. She stressed that 'there was nothing odd or gloomy in the choice of *Waiting for Godot*', but that 'Beckett's play, written over forty years ago, seems written for and about Sarajevo' (Sontag 1993, 52). Explaining her decision further, she argued that the play was

> about abandoned people, weak, vulnerable people, waiting for something to happen that they go on hoping against hope will happen, and yet it's perfectly clear it's not going to happen and that's the situation of the people of Sarajevo. (Oppenheim 1995, 38)

Tickets were free for the Sarajevans who risked incoming mortars and snipers' bullets to attend the show, which took place in the relative safety of the afternoon. Conditions were far from routine in the theatre itself. The stage, on two levels (Pozzo and Lucky performed on a raised upstage platform), was lit by only twelve candles and some meagre solar lamps and was littered with the paraphernalia of the immediate outside world: sandbags, rope, polyurethane sheeting, humanitarian aid crates and the detritus of the repeatedly shelled streets. In this context, certain of Sontag's directorial decisions were clearly dictated by practicalities. Only one of the play's two acts, for example, constituted the entire performance. Clearly there was a necessity for brevity for reasons of safety and comfort, but Sontag also stated: 'Perhaps I felt that the despair of Act I was enough for the Sarajevo audience, and that I wanted to spare them a second time when Godot does not arrive. Maybe I wanted to propose, subliminally, that Act II might be different' (Sontag 1993, 56).

While the play was lopped in half, such economy did not apply to its casting, which involved multiples of the original characters (there were also two trees). The Vladimir/Estragon pairing was tripled, with three actors playing each role; one couple was male, one female, and one comprised a male and a female actor. Pozzo was female while Lucky was male, and the child was performed by an adult actor. This cast and the production crew represented the multicultural city from which they hailed: Muslim and Christian, Bosnian, Serb and Croatian.

The multiple casting served numerous functions; while the mixed ethnicity articulated an ideologically liberal vision of unity that spoke to the immediate political background, the manner in which the pairs interacted within each unit of two, or between these units, was informed by both the thematic substance of the play and by the context of the production. To start with, each Vladimir/Estragon couple took turns to utter Beckett's words, maintaining a sense of dialogue between two distinct characters despite their multiple manifestations. As such, they offered a picture of a fragmented community, each pair isolated from the other two. By the end of the single act all the characters acknowledged the others, speaking almost as a chorus of Didis and Gogos, having become a single, united 'community' sharing the same plight and hopes. 'By the time Pozzo is eating', Erika Munk recalled, 'the Didis and Gogos have become the chorus Sontag wanted, Lucky and Pozzo's audience, and a hungry, rebellious population' (Munk 1993, 26).

In entering a war zone and arranging this production, Sontag undoubtedly performed a brave act of solidarity with the citizens of Sarajevo seeking, through art, to offer some modest but powerful 'expression of human dignity – which is what the people of Sarajevo feel they have lost' (Sontag 2002, 304).

There is no record of Beckett's response, if any, to the presentation of his text in Israel. Sontag's production was four years after his death, and in such circumstances that any intervention by the Beckett Estate would have been unthinkable. Beckett scholars, however, have taken issue with these productions, with the most critical attention focused on the Sarajevan reduction of the play and multiplying of the characters (see Oppenheim 1995, for example). To criticize 'abuses' of Beckett's text is to subscribe to the notion (supported in some ways by legislation) that the cultural event that might occur from the use of a text requires a fastidious respect for the text that inspires that event. Alternatively, one might accept that to enter into dialogue with a written text, and to do so through rehearsal and performance, is to recognize possibilities and variants that the processes of creative inspiration and cultural circumstances might bring to the fore. These last two 'ideotextual' *mises en scène* of *Waiting for Godot* offer food for thought on the degree to which it is legitimate to enter into such dialogue with an author's text, and on the degree to which such an approach is a service or a disservice to its author.

# 4 Workshopping the Play

## Page to stage

The text of *Waiting for Godot* that you hold in your hand is a literary artefact. As we have done, you can apply literary analyses to it in order to interrogate it and attempt to come to conclusions as to its worth, its 'message', its expressivity and how its formal structure participates in rendering such things to the reader. While such an approach might offer up legitimate readings of the literary manifestation of the play (the text) they do not necessarily hold the same worth in thinking about a live manifestation of the play (the performance). As a member of an audience, different combinations of intellectual and emotional responses are stimulated and one employs different faculties in addressing and responding to what one witnesses than when perusing a script. Put simply, you 'read' it differently. These two modes of reading any play are of course mutually informing, and adopting both approaches when studying a work of drama is the most profitable way of accessing the work. Doing practical work with the text, then, is an alternative and useful way of asking questions of it.

This chapter offers a series of practical workshop exercises and prompts for discussion that may be of use to students or actors studying Beckett's most famous text. These are structured purposefully to separate intellectual discussion from more practical approaches. While intellectual discussion is useful in achieving an overview of the play and how it operates, it can also interfere with more practical approaches. For example, excessive discussion in the rehearsal room can impede progress in that context just as forming too rigid an interpretation from having read a play, and about it, can unhelpfully constrain how to approach character practically. Beckett himself warned against the tendency to intellectualize his work. In a letter to his American director Alan Schneider, who had asked him for some information about the characters in his play *Endgame*, he replied:

> My work is a matter of fundamental sounds (no joke intended) made as fully as possible, and I accept responsibility for nothing else. If people want to have headaches among the overtones, let them. And provide their own aspirin. (Harmon 1998, 24)

Beckett, here, makes it clear that as an artist he takes responsibility only for the basic structures (the 'fundamental sounds') that his plays evoke, the shapes of human experience that they conjure. Critics and audiences may well give themselves 'headaches' with all their intellectualizing, and they may well need to prescribe themselves the 'aspirin' of answers and solutions to the questions they have raised. For Beckett, however, both the questions and the answers – the 'headaches' and the 'aspirin' – are irrelevant to that which he sought to achieve. The 'joke' concerning fundamental sounds is a reference to belching and farting, behaviour which comically punctuates a lot of Beckett's writing. This joke may not have been as unintended as Beckett claims, as he may have meant mischievously to equate the hot air of intellectual discussion to those other gaseous expulsions.

As we have discussed, Beckett's plays (and much of his prose) are concerned with the human appetite for meaning. He charts this appetite specifically in relation to our being, to our sense of identity, and how our behaviour seems centred around finding justifications for our being alive. He maps how we seek stable grounds for a sense of personal identity, and want to prove to ourselves (or fool ourselves) that our sense of self is reliable, constant and knowable.

He demonstrates the frustrating instability and elusiveness of such a position of certainty. Given this fundamental attribute in his writing, it is ironic that as students of his work we seek to want to define it, pin it down, be certain about it – to achieve the very thing that the work denies is possible. This fact of a human appetite for 'meaning' is our starting point, and offers us two perspectives from which to begin in the rehearsal room or class workshop: (*a*) that Beckett's work, in frustrating us, is operating on us effectively. It is making us feel the very thing it is seeking to express, rather than trying to tell us in any conventional way; (*b*) that we should be wary of any sense that we have 'got it', and instead value uncertainty, especially with regard to the effective portrayal of Beckett's theatre.

Discussion and practical work might begin around achieving an understanding of what Beckett means by 'fundamental sounds'. Rather than being merely dismissive of Schneider's request, his letter to the director gives away something of Beckett's artistic credo and reminds us of what he told the critic Harold Hobson in 1956: 'I am interested in the shape of ideas [. . .] It is the shape that matters' (see page 32). Perhaps the 'shape' that an idea adopts, concretized in real movement, gesture and rhythm on stage, is the mode by which an audience can digest what is in front of them via a process of recognition. Perhaps this is a theatre in which 'fundamental sounds' resonate within us, if properly sounded by the actors and the design, to evoke an awareness of what is being spoken that eludes, or does not require, articulation.

Beckett's theatre, then, offers a conundrum for actors. On stage, an actor needs to feel he or she knows who or what they are representing, and, through rehearsal, needs to acquire a sense of some stable identity that they are representing. *Waiting for Godot* undermines the very basis of such stability and its actors need to consider their characters as integrated elements in a larger set of aesthetic patterns. The following three sets of exercises and prompts for discussion aim to offer some preliminary ways in which such a task might be begun. Using three excerpts from the text, they aim to consider the 'shapes' and 'fundamental sounds' of the play rather than to entertain notions of characterization, motivation and 'backstory'. They also encourage participants to consider ways of expressing the themes of the play through the relationships developed between characters. In what follows we have separated discussion about the play from 'rehearsal' exercises, which aim to facilitate a practical examination of the drama.

## 1 – Vladimir and Estragon

The first section of the play to be considered is a passage of 'waiting' and of dialogue between the two key protagonists. The excerpt begins in Act II on p. 67 with Vladimir's question to Estragon 'Where are your boots?' and finishes on p. 71 with the exchange 'Let's go / We can't / Why not? / We're waiting for Godot / Ah!'

The exercise can be done in pairs, or in small groups with some observing pairs, or with the class separated in a large room into groups of paired Vladimirs and Estragons. This work in pairs is more successful if the lines have been learned before the workshop, but works effectively nonetheless with scripts in hands.

### Workshop

Begin with a seated read-through of the section, out loud, in order to familiarize yourselves with progression and events within it. Do this even if you have learned the lines by heart for the exercise, as this will give you an opportunity to reconsider the fall of the lines immediately before having to think about performing them.

Draw or imagine a line on the studio floor separating a 'stage' space into two (a whole studio might be separated in two for larger groups). One half of this space should be labelled (or simply remembered) to represent 'worry' and the other 'avoiding worry'.

The rules of the exercise are simple: The further away from the line an actor stands into the 'worry' half, the more worried s/he feels. The further away from the line s/he stands in the 'avoiding worry' side, the more distracted s/he is from that worry. It does not matter what is 'worrying' the actor in the role, and the exercise works best if nothing particular is imagined, for now.

Start the section with both actors standing on the line. The actors should not be concerned about inhabiting a real or imagined stage space at this point – there is no tree, no boots, no location for them to imagine around them, just abstract notions of 'worry' and 'avoiding worry'. So, for example, when they talk of boots, they do not act out the trying on of boots, they just utter the words and consider whether those lines are an impulse to worry, or facilitate an avoidance of worry. Similarly, when the text indicates that the actors are together, as when Vladimir sings Estragon to sleep, the actors should avoid acting this out. The actors are simply expressing the lines in open space.

The actors start in the centre of the studio and recite or read out their lines, one at a time. If a line indicates to the actor speaking it that the character is concerned, bothered, upset or angry, s/he should take a step towards or into the 'worry' section of the space. If, instead, the line seems to be avoiding such emotions, s/he should step towards or into the 'avoiding worry' section.

Consequent lines might push the actor further into one section s/he already occupies, or pull him/her towards the other section. When no such impulse can be felt, the actor stays still as s/he delivers that line. Actors can only take a pace or two at a time. If, for instance, an actor is deep within 'worry' territory, and feel that a line offers 'avoiding worry', s/he can only move towards that part of the space, like a King on a chess board, not cross over in one full set of strides like the Queen.

It is important to remember that, as an actor, you are responding to what the text gives you, not attempting to apply an interpretation to it. That is to say, follow the impulse of what the line seems to indicate, and avoid trying to apply a possible alternative to the line at this stage. It might be useful to break the section down into segments to complete this exercise, and to do each separately, stopping to discuss the decisions that have been made.

The exercise might then be repeated, but replacing 'worry' and 'avoiding worry' with 'love' and 'hate'. This time, the actors would move in accord with whether they felt their line was an expression of affection for the other, or of irritation towards the other.

Finally, a line might be drawn (or imagined) across the first line, cutting the space into quarters. The impulses of 'worry', 'avoiding worry', 'love' and 'hate' might now be placed at the ends of those lines, so that the gravitational movements out from the centre might be up towards 'worry', up right towards 'worry/hate', up left towards 'worry/love', down left towards 'avoiding worry/love' and so on.

Remember, the actors respond to their individual lines, not to each other. So, for example, it is quite possible that when Vladimir is sending Estragon to sleep, the two actors might be in different quadrants of the space, and at opposite ends of the rehearsal room.

**Discussion**
When the actors have run through the scene in each of these ways, they might want to look back and see how they have got to where they are standing in the space, and discuss what moves took them there. They may have made notes as they did the exercise, or witnesses might have taken detailed notes, and/or maps, of how the actors moved within the grid. Consider any general inclinations to move in any direction, and what implication that might have on an interpretation of the text. Was there a wavering between halves (or quadrants) of the space or did they find themselves moving more and more into 'worry' territory, for example? Did they find themselves moving in one direction for a part of the excerpt, and then away again for the rest? The actors should discuss between themselves, or with members of the rest of the group, what patterns their movements described. For example, in the first exercise with the space divided in half, what proportion of the time did each actor

spend in (or moving towards) the 'worry' section? What lines put them further into it, and what lines moved them out of it? Discuss why those lines perhaps contributed to those inclinations. When the 'love/hate' axis was added, was it possible to determine a correlation between the characters' waxing and waning affection, and the degree to which they manifest worry? Did the degree to which the character manifested affection for his companion correlate at all to the degree to which he was 'avoiding worry'? What of distractions such as the boot? Rather than playing the scene with the boot-trying for laughs, to what degree does this exercise indicate to you that the distraction serves a thematic purpose?

Once you have had this discussion, you might then be able to consider which lines generated 'worry' and articulate what it is that the character is or might be worried about. Similarly, you could discuss the dynamics of the two characters' friendship as laid out by their motion to and fro across the 'love/hate' axis, and see what patterns of behaviour might be defined in terms of how they express affection or manifest need from one another. You might wish to repeat the exercise after your discussion, to consolidate and 'learn' the impulses you have identified. Then, with these in mind, you might try to rehearse the scene more naturally: forget the rules of the game and respond directly to one another, but remember how 'love', 'hate', 'worry' and 'avoiding worry' wax and wane in the scene, and see how your awareness of these movements affect how the characters interact in rehearsal. So, for example, if you agree that the exercise indicated to you that there were some very clear impulses away from one mood to another, refer to these as 'impulse moments' and consider how you might manifest them in more traditional rehearsal of the excerpt – with a strong gesture, perhaps, or an extended piece of movement (crossing the stage), or with verbal emphasis.

You could of course choose very different axes to use in this exercise instead of, or in addition to, the suggested ones relating to worry or affection. Your choice of axes should be informed by your understanding of the themes of the play. By applying opposing tensions in this way, you are effectively asking questions of the text in a practical way, as though putting it through a filter to see what does not work and passes through and what residue remains for you to then consider further in rehearsing the scene.

## 2 – Vladimir, Estragon, Pozzo and Lucky

The segment under focus here is the section of the play that immediately precedes Lucky's speech in Act I. It begins on p. 38 with Pozzo's enquiry 'How did you find me?' and ends with his instruction to 'Think, pig!' a few pages later, before Lucky opens his mouth.

This series of exercises can be carried out by students in groups of four, with each taking one of the four onstage characters.

### Workshop

Begin in groups with a quick read-through of the piece, even if it has been already learned by heart, to familiarize yourselves with what is said in it, and how it progresses. As with the first set of exercises above, there is no need to visualize or create a 'real' stage space with a tree and so on. With this exercise, the actors are more likely and able to acknowledge and interact with one another than in the previous set of exercises.

The short section is going to be performed four times. Each time, a different character will stand in the centre, with the other three around him. Lucky's role, of course, is silent, but he should be present to be acknowledged in the scenario, and to be spoken to or about by the other actors.

The actor who is in the centre speaks his/her lines, but adds a clause each time s/he speaks that describes what the character might be trying to achieve with his line. The clause would begin 'he said' and end with an adverb that describes the manner in which the character might have intended to speak the line. So, for example, the actor playing Vladimir, when s/he is in the centre, instead of simply saying 'Oh very good, very very good', might say 'Oh very good, very very good, he said sycophantically'.

When not in the centre, the other actors simply deliver their lines unembellished. One by one, then, the actors each take turns in doing the scene but with one of them adding the adverbs, putting their own character under focus. Actors can move towards and away from one another, and touch one another, but the actor in the centre must remain roughly in between all the other characters.

When it is Lucky's turn, there needs to be a new rule, as the character has no lines in the chosen section. After every three lines spoken by the other characters, Lucky puts up his hand to speak, and says 'I want to . . .' followed by a response based upon what he is hearing. Try to avoid repeating any of Lucky's desires, but try to keep focussed on what he might be thinking in response to what he is hearing, especially when the other three are talking about him.

In order to capture the actors' decisions as they each in turn respond to the lines allocated to them, it is a good idea to take notes as you do the exercise, or to have someone else taking notes as they listen.

### Discussion

The purpose of this exercise is twofold: it permits actors space to think about the impulses behind their lines and consider how those develop within the scene, and it also helps us to better consider what status Lucky has as a character, and how status is being negotiated or articulated among all four characters. Though the actor playing Lucky has no lines, s/he benefits from considering what his/her character's responses might be to being spoken about and told what to do. As the other characters articulate their relationship with Lucky (in terms of what they stand to benefit from him, and how they feel about that) the actor playing Lucky has an opportunity to consider how this might affect his/her interpretation of the role, and to think of what Lucky's investment is in his apparently willing subjugation. Discuss these relationships, and consider specifically these matters: (*a*) Pozzo's attitude to Lucky, (*b*) Pozzo's attitude to Vladimir and Estragon, (*c*) Vladimir and Estragon's attitudes to Pozzo, and whether they differ or are the same, or vary through the section, and (*d*) Lucky's attitude to his situation, and to the manner in which he is objectified and treated by the other three. In extending the discussion, you might discuss how these attitudes change when Pozzo and Lucky return in Act II, and, if you have the time, you could repeat the exercise using an excerpt from that later section of the play.

### 3 – Vladimir, Estragon and the boy

The section of the play used for the final series of exercises is the closing section of Act II. Starting from the entrance of the boy on p. 91 and his line 'Mister . . . Mister Albert', take the last pages of the play up to the curtain. This passage is in two sections: the discussion between Vladimir and the boy, during which Estragon is asleep, and the final moments between Vladimir and Estragon. These two sections can be worked upon separately at first. The work can be done either in pairs, sharing the three roles (Estragon and the boy never share dialogue with Vladimir), or in groups of three.

### Workshop

Starting with the first segment between Vladimir and the boy, run the brief scene four times. The first time, Vladimir should use the line 'Off we go again' as an incitement to anger, and demonstrate impatience and cynicism in his dealings with the boy. In the second run-through, he should use the phrase as indicative of his resignation, and play his part sad, unsurprised by the boy's answers. On the third run-through he should be angry once more and on the fourth resigned once more. On the first two runs the boy should be afraid of Vladimir, and on the third and fourth he should be nonchalant, monosyllabic, unconcerned with Vladimir's questions and simply carrying out a boring errand that means nothing to him.

The person performing Vladimir should at this stage resist asking why his character might be angry or resigned, and not worry about his/her 'motivation' for doing so. The exercise simply requires that the actor apply that mood to the lines, even when it might seem to jar with individual phrases. Similarly, the actor taking the part of the boy should just apply the given response, and not be concerned if this doesn't seem to be the right way of doing the section. This is because the exercise is not immediately seeking to identify the 'correct' mode of delivery, but examining specific colours in the palette to see which of their tones could apply and where.

Once the first part of the scene has been dealt with, now rehearse the final section, starting with Estragon waking as Vladimir stands, bowed, downstage from him. Again, run it four times: twice with Vladimir carrying the residue of his anger, and twice with him carrying the residue of his resignation from the scene with the boy. Let the actor playing Estragon respond as s/he sees fit in the circumstances, but the third and fourth times through, s/he should try actively to reverse Vladimir's mood with the given lines. Once you have gone through all the permutations, join the two sections together to run the full scene four times. The four runs of the scene would therefore be:

First run: Vladimir angry, boy afraid of Vladimir, Estragon responds as he wishes.

Second run: Vladimir resigned, boy nonchalant, Estragon responds as he wishes.

Third run: Vladimir angry, boy nonchalant, Estragon trying to calm Vladimir.

Fourth run: Vladimir resigned, boy afraid of Vladimir, Estragon trying to cheer Vladimir up.

There are other possible attitudes and combinations to adopt or try in rehearsal, of course, but these seem suitable matches in the first instance. You might discuss which others to try in further applications of the exercise.

**Discussion**

As you run the four proposed versions of the scene, make notes after each about which lines seemed to work with the suggested moods applied. If there are witnesses to the four run-throughs, it would be useful if they could note down where they think these applied moods worked best, and where they didn't seem to work. Note and discuss any responses the actor playing Estragon felt inclined to make in the first two runs and how successful they seemed. The actors might also wish to note where the given mood seemed utterly at odds with the given lines.

After running all four versions, discuss what seemed to work best and why. Relate your responses to what you understand of the play's themes, and how Vladimir and Estragon feel an obligation to wait, a need to wait and a weariness at waiting for something that will help define them and their lives. Try to discuss and agree on a balance between what you feel works best as actors, and what is most appropriate in terms of your understanding of the play's themes. Return to the scene and run it again, this time using aspects of what you agreed worked for certain lines. So, for example, you might think that Vladimir moves from anger to resignation during the course of the scene, and that Estragon joins him in resignation, moves to despair, but attempts to cheer up his friend. Run the scene with those variations and progressions and then discuss how that works, whether it serves the play's themes and whether the two characters give each other enough by way of response to justify those developments. If you cannot agree on a permutation of variations and progressions, try the alternative ones that are suggested and discuss them from the perspective of the actor, and of the audience.

You can then attempt to apply a different set of moods to the scene and start the exercise from scratch with these. Or, you can use anger again, but replace resignation with despair. It can even be useful to do this exercise using moods that do not at first seem appropriate to the scene, such as hilarity or scorn. By running the scene with a variety of palettes of mood applied to the lines, it can be remarkable which moods seem to 'stick' and seem appropriate to the delivery of certain lines. This can serve as a means of shining a torch into corners of the scene to learn more about what the text offers to actors.

Beckett originally explained to Peter Hall that Vladimir's final lines should be spoken with a 'dead numb tone' (Harmon 1998, 5). Discuss this after you have done this exercise. Do you understand why Beckett might have wanted a colourless vocal response from Vladimir? What benefit would this have, and how does it compare to the kinds of delivery that your Vladimir tried out?

The three sets of exercises offered here, and the associated prompts for discussion, are examples of the kind of approach to the text that one might make in early rehearsal or when wishing to ask questions of it in a practical manner. They are not exhaustive – many other exercises of this type could equally well be applied. One of the objectives of the approach here is to avoid the kinds of discussion and exercises that are often employed with more conventional play scripts, for which issues of character and the development of narrative are more central to the development of the play in practice. Another objective is to avoid bringing interpretations to the text too early, and instead to trust Beckett's words, and see what they inspire when being uttered, when activated as dialogue as opposed to being simply read off the page. We hope they prove useful, as some straightforward ways of interrogating this most indefinable but rewarding of plays.

# Timeline 1945–55

## 1945

| Politics | Culture |
| --- | --- |
| End of the Second World War; United States uses atomic weapons against Japan; Clement Atlee's Labour government replaces Winston Churchill's wartime coalition; the trials of major war criminals begin in Nuremburg, Germany | *Animal Farm* by George Orwell published; The BBC's light programme is broadcast on the radio; David Lean's *Brief Encounter* released; novelist André Malraux is appointed Minister of Information by de Gaulle in France |

## 1946

| | |
| --- | --- |
| Winston Churchill coins the phrase 'Iron Curtain' in an anti-Soviet speech; the UN Security Council meets for the first time | *An Inspector Calls* by J. B. Priestley first performed; Bikinis are sold for the first time in Paris; B. B. King and Dean Martin begin recording careers |

## 1947

| | |
| --- | --- |
| India and Pakistan achieve independence from British rule; over 4000 Jewish Holocaust survivors leave France for Palestine on board the Exodus; there are localized riots in France when the personal bread ration is lowered; US Marshall plan offers aid to Europe; start of the French Fourth Republic | French designer Christian Dior introduces the New Look, which defines the fashions of the post-war years; the Edinburgh International Festival begins; the Dead Sea scrolls are discovered; the *Diary of Ann Frank* published; Jean Genet's *Les Bonnes* (*The Maids*) staged in Paris by Louis Jouvet; Albert Camus's *La Peste* (*The Plague*) published |

## 1948

| Politics | Culture |
|----------|---------|
| Mahatma Gandhi is assassinated in India; the Soviet Union stops road and rail travel between Berlin and western Germany, forcing the Western powers to organize a massive airlift, heightening Cold War tensions; the State of Israel comes into being; the British National Health Service is established | English academic F. R. Leavis publishes *The Great Tradition*, an influential analysis of the importance of the English novel; Antonin Artaud dies in his clinic room in Paris; Laurence Olivier's film version of *Hamlet* is released and wins an Oscar; The BBC broadcasts a debate between philosophers Bertrand Russell and Frederick Copleston on the existence of God |

## 1949

| | |
|----------|---------|
| Soviet Union explodes its first atomic bomb; NATO is established; Ireland declared a republic | *A Streetcar Named Desire* by Tennessee Williams first performed in London; *Nineteen Eighty-Four* by George Orwell published; *Death of a Salesman* by Arthur Miller opens in New York; Rodgers and Hammerstein's *South Pacific* opens on Broadway; Jean-Paul Sartre's *The Roads to Freedom* trilogy completed |

## 1950

| | |
|----------|---------|
| American senator Joe McCarthy begins an anti-Communist 'witch-hunt'; the British General Election has an 84 per cent turnout but Labour gains only slim majority and calls another election | The comic strip *Peanuts*, featuring Charlie Brown and his dog Snoopy, is first printed in the United States; Eugène Ionesco's *La Cantatrice Chauve* (*The Bald Prima Donna*) is staged in Paris |

## 1951

| Politics | Culture |
| --- | --- |
| Conservative Party wins General Election and 77-year-old Winston Churchill becomes prime minister | _Relative Values_ by Noël Coward first performed; film of Tennessee Williams's _A Streetcar Named Desire_, starring Marlon Brando, released; J. Sainsbury opens his first supermarket |

## 1952

| | |
| --- | --- |
| Britain produces its own atomic bomb; United States tests the first hydrogen bomb; George VI dies and is succeeded by his daughter Elizabeth II | _The Deep Blue Sea_ by Terence Rattigan first performed; Agatha Christie's _The Mousetrap_ opens in London to begin an uninterrupted run for the rest of the century and beyond; Arthur Adamov's _La Parodie_ (_The Parody_) mounted by Roger Blin in Paris |

## 1953

| | |
| --- | --- |
| Coronation of Queen Elizabeth II; Josef Stalin, Soviet dictator, dies; Soviet Union tests hydrogen bomb | _The Wild One_, film starring Marlon Brando, released; CBS begins first colour television broadcasts in the United States; broadcast of the Queen's coronation on TV causes a huge increase in TV ownership in Britain; Ian Fleming publishes his first James Bond novel, _Casino Royale_ |

## 1954

| Politics | Culture |
| --- | --- |
| United States tests the hydrogen bomb in Bikini Atoll; wartime rationing of food finally ends in Britain; The eight-year Algerian War of Independence against France begins | *Lucky Jim* by Kingsley Amis published; *Separate Tables* by Terence Rattigan first performed; *On the Waterfront* released; *Lord of the Flies* by William Golding published; *Lord of the Rings* by J. R. R. Tolkien; American rock 'n' roll musician Bill Haley releases 'Rock Around the Clock'; first portable transistor radios are marketed; Kenneth Tynan becomes theatre critic of the *Observer* |

## 1955

| Politics | Culture |
| --- | --- |
| Winston Churchill resigns as British prime minister due to ill health and is replaced by Anthony Eden; The Republic of Ireland joins the United Nations | Commercial television introduced in Britain; American film-maker Nicholas Ray's *Rebel without a Cause*, starring popular icon James Dean, released; Russian-American novelist Vladimir Nabokov publishes *Lolita* in Paris; first Disney theme park opens in California; *Guinness Book of Records* first published |

# Notes

## Chapter 1: Background and Context

1. The anonymous critic of the Arts journal referred to both *Waiting for Godot* and another play, in the title of his unsigned review: 'Au Babylone et au Lancry - Deux coups heureux sur le damier du théâtre' (*Arts*, 16 January 1953). The title does not translate unawkwardly: 'At the Babylone and Lancry theatres – Two welcome strikes knocking the dust off the theatre'. The 'strikes' in question are the strikes people used to make with a stick against rugs hung over washing lines to remove dust as part of regular housecleaning chores.

2. The titles in English became *Mercier and Camier, Molloy, Malone Dies, The Unnamable, Eleutheria* and, of course, *Waiting for Godot*. The English titles will be used from this point forward. All quotations will be from the English editions, except where indicated.

3. See Graver (70–8) for a useful summary of key differences between the French and the English *Waiting for Godot*.

## Chapter 2: Analysis and Commentary

1. Unless otherwise indicated, all translations are by the authors of this book.

2. In the updated English text this reference became 'Adam' (37).

3. Jean Cocteau demanded that 'poetry in the theatre' (dialogue-based drama) be replaced by 'poetry of the theatre' in his preface to *The Wedding on the Eiffel Tower* (Cocteau, 67). Antonin Artaud proposed that one facet of such a theatre would involve 'a new bodily language [which is] no longer based on words but on signs which emerge through the maze of gestures, postures, airborne cries' creating actors who became 'moving hieroglyphs' (Artaud, 37).

4. A 'grand narrative' can be religious, scientific, historical, sociological, moral, aesthetic – the term is deliberately general in order to denote a type of 'narrative' rather than any specific one. The word 'narrative' in this context does not mean 'story', but might represent any structural system that we adopt as normative or which we regard as authoritative, such as a political system, a

subscription to class or caste distinctions, a collection of cultural assumptions, and so on.

## Chapter 3: Production History

1. The full details of this audience survey to the Haifa production are presented and analysed in Soshana Weitz, 'Mr Godot will not come today'.

# Further Reading

There is a vast (and ever-growing) amount of criticism on Beckett, and especially on *Waiting for Godot*. The following bibliography does not attempt to be exhaustive and we have not included individual articles or book chapters on Beckett, or more specialized critical studies. What follows is a selected list of suggested further reading aimed at students and those who are relatively new to Beckett's work. More advanced and detailed bibliographical guides can be found in Boxall, Oppenheim and Pattie (details below).

## Editions of *Waiting for Godot*

Beckett, Samuel (1952), *En attendant Godot*. Paris: Éditions de Minuit. The original French version of the play.

Beckett, Samuel (1965), *Waiting for Godot*. London: Faber and Faber. All references in this book are to this edition, except where stated.

Knowlson, James (ed.) (1993), *The Theatrical Notebooks of Samuel Beckett. Volume 1: Waiting for Godot*. London: Faber and Faber. Considered by many to offer the definitive edition of the play, with extensive annotations, notes and a facsimile and annotated transcript of Beckett's production notebook for his 1975 Schiller-Theater production.

## Books about *Waiting for Godot*

Bradby, David (2001), *Plays in Production: 'Waiting for Godot'*. Cambridge: Cambridge University Press. An excellent book, which includes a particularly useful overview chapter on the play and a critical survey of productions of the play.

Cohn, Ruby (ed.) (1987), *Samuel Beckett: 'Waiting for Godot': A Casebook*. Basingstoke: Macmillan. A useful collection of reviews, early criticism, and extracts from essays on a range of topics.

Connor, Steven (ed.) (1992), *'Waiting for Godot' and 'Endgame'*. Basingstoke: Macmillan. Part of the 'New Casebooks' series, this updates Cohn's earlier Casebook, providing a collection of more recent theoretical approaches to the plays.

Gordon, Lois G. (2002), *Reading Godot*. New Haven, CT: Yale University Press. Presents interesting and detailed analyses of the play in the context of existentialism and Freudian theory.

Graver, Lawrence (2004), *Samuel Beckett: 'Waiting for Godot'* (2nd edn). Cambridge: Cambridge University Press. An introductory overview of the play and its context, which includes some excellent close analysis of the text.

Worth, Katharine (1990), *'Waiting for Godot' and 'Happy Days': Text and Performance*, Basingstoke: Macmillan. A useful introduction to the plays, which provides a combination of textual close reading and analysis of individual productions.

## Biographies

Bair, Deirdre (1990), *Samuel Beckett: A Biography*. London: Vintage. The first Beckett biography, which has since been criticized for containing some inaccuracies.

Brater, Enoch (2003), *The Essential Samuel Beckett: An Illustrated Biography*. London: Thames and Hudson. Previously published in an earlier edition in 1989 as *Why Beckett* (London: Thames and Hudson, 1989). A concise, accessible and fully illustrated guide to Beckett's life and work.

Cronin, Anthony (1997), *Samuel Beckett: The Last Modernist.* London: Flamingo. A readable account of Beckett's life and achievement that places him in his literary contexts.

Knowlson, James (1997), *Damned to Fame: The Life of Samuel Beckett.* London: Bloomsbury. The definitive and authorized biography of Beckett. Detailed, scholarly, and insightful.

## General studies of Beckett

Acheson, James (1997), *Samuel Beckett's Artistic Theory and Practice: Criticism, Drama and Early Fiction.* Basingstoke: Macmillan. Places Beckett's plays and fiction in the context of his writings on art and literature. Includes part of a chapter on *Waiting for Godot*, examining the balance between tragedy and comedy in the play.

Ben-Zvi, Linda (1986), *Samuel Beckett.* Boston: Twayne Publishers. A chronological survey of Beckett's work from his early criticism to his later prose and dramatic works.

Cohn, Ruby (1973), *Back to Beckett.* Princeton: Princeton University Press. A concise survey of all of Beckett's writing.

Cohn, Ruby (1980), *Just Play: Beckett's Theater.* Princeton: Princeton University Press. Considers Beckett's theatre, first by offering analytical material, then by considering the pieces in production before concentrating on Beckett's own work as a director.

Cohn, Ruby (1987), *From Desire to Godot.* Los Angeles: University of California Press. An account of specific productions of the avant-garde fringe theatres in post-war Paris, including a chapter on the first production of Beckett's play.

Cohn, Ruby (2001), *A Beckett Canon.* Ann Arbor: University of Michigan Press. A valuable companion to reading all genres of Beckett's output. Concentrates on the original language versions of his works, with appendices on Beckett's translations and productions.

Connor, Steven (1988), *Samuel Beckett: Repetition, Theory and Text*. Oxford: Blackwell. Examines Beckett's preoccupation with repetition in relation to post-structuralism. Includes a short but very interesting section on *Waiting for Godot* and *Endgame*.

Esslin, Martin (1968), *The Theatre of the Absurd*. Harmondsworth: Penguin. Situates Beckett within an artificial school of writers, including Arthur Adamov, Eugène Ionesco and Jean Genet, each of whom addressed existential concerns or issues of problematized subjectivity. A very influential early study.

Fletcher, Beryl S. and Fletcher, John (1985), *A Student's Guide to the Plays of Samuel Beckett* (2nd edn). London: Faber and Faber. Includes a brief essay on *Waiting for Godot*, and some useful annotations to the text of the play.

Fletcher, John and Spurling, John (1985), *Beckett the Playwright* (3rd edn). Introductory overview of Beckett's plays, including a good chapter on *Waiting for Godot*.

Fletcher, John (2000), Samuel Beckett: '*Waiting for Godot*', '*Krapp's Last Tape*' and '*Endgame*'. London: Faber and Faber. Very concise but authoritative students' guide to these Beckett plays.

Fletcher, John (2003), *About Beckett: The Playwright and the Work*. London: Faber and Faber. Places Beckett's plays in their literary and cultural context. Includes a very useful survey of interviews with Beckett and his collaborators and of Beckett's work as a director.

Graver, Lawrence and Federman, Raymond (1979), *Samuel Beckett: The Critical Heritage*. London: Routledge. A useful collection of contemporary reviews and critical responses to Beckett's work. Includes a number of reviews of the first productions of *Waiting for Godot*.

Kennedy, Andrew (1989), *Samuel Beckett*. Cambridge: Cambridge University Press. Part of the 'British and Irish Authors Introductory Critical Studies'. Provides a good survey and introductory overview of Beckett's major works, focusing on a selection of stage plays and Beckett's trilogy of novels (*Molloy, Malone Dies, The Unnamable*).

Knowlson, James and Knowlson, Elizabeth (2006), *Beckett Remembering, Remembering Beckett: Uncollected Interviews with Samuel Beckett and Memories of Those Who Knew Him*. London: Bloomsbury. A collection of interviews with Samuel Beckett, and with those who were close to him or who worked with him. As such, a valuable resource.

McDonald, Rónán (2006), *The Cambridge Introduction to Samuel Beckett*. Cambridge: Cambridge University Press. An accessible and well-written introduction, which provides a very useful introductory overview of Beckett's life and work.

McMillan, Dougald and Fehsenfeld, Martha (1988), *Beckett in the Theatre: The Author as Practical Playwright and Director. Volume 1: From 'Waiting for Godot' to 'Krapp's Last Tape'*. London: John Calder. A useful resource that compiles a variety of documentary sources and eye-witness accounts of Beckett's own rehearsal room activity.

Oppenheim, Lois (ed.) (1994), *Directing Beckett*, Ann Arbor: University of Michigan Press. A collection of fascinating interviews and essays with and by those who have collaborated with Beckett, or who are artistically associated with his work, on the subject of the performance of his unique brand of theatre.

Pattie, David (2000), *The Complete Critical Guide to Samuel Beckett*. A very good introductory overview of Beckett's life and work, and of critical responses to Beckett. Entries on individual texts are necessarily brief, but the book's comprehensive coverage makes it particularly useful for students who want to gain a general overview of Beckett's oeuvre.

Pilling, John (ed.) (1994), *The Cambridge Companion to Beckett*. Cambridge: Cambridge University Press. A collection of essays covering all of Beckett's oeuvre, including an insightful chapter by Michael Worton on *Waiting for Godot* and *Endgame*.

## Reference guides

Ackerley, C. J. and Gontarski, S. E. (2006), *The Faber Companion to Samuel Beckett*. London: Faber and Faber. A wonderfully detailed and varied alphabetic reference guide, which provides clear and succinct entries on a very wide range of texts and topics. Previously published in the US as *The Grove Companion to Samuel Beckett*, New York: Grove Press.

Hutchings, William (2005), *Samuel Beckett's 'Waiting for Godot': A Reference Guide*. Connecticut: Prager. Contains a thorough list of productions of *Waiting for Godot*.

Pilling, John (2006), *A Samuel Beckett Chronology*. Basingstoke: Palgrave Macmillan. A thorough and detailed chronology of Beckett's life, citing events, movements and correspondence.

## Guides to Beckett criticism

Boxall, Peter (2000), *Samuel Beckett, 'Waiting for Godot'/'Endgame': A Reader's Guide to Essential Criticism*. Cambridge: Icon Books. A survey of critical responses to Beckett's first two plays, arranged chronologically, from early responses, through liberal humanist readings to the more recent application of critical theory and ideological readings.

Oppenheim, Lois (ed.) (2004), *Palgrave Advances in Samuel Beckett Studies*. Houndmills, Basingstoke: Palgrave Macmillan. A useful and detailed guide to Beckett criticism. Contains chapters by leading Beckett scholars examining key critical and theoretical debates in Beckett studies.

## Websites

'The Samuel Beckett Endpage', www.ua.ac.be/beckett/.
    Hosted by the University of Antwerp, and edited by Dirk Van Hulle. Contains information about Beckett, news and

information about publications and performances, and also houses the official home page of the Samuel Beckett Society.

'Apmonia: A Site for Samuel Beckett', www.themodernword.com/beckett/.

This site is part of the excellent literary website 'The Modern Word', and is edited by Tim Conley and Allen Ruch. It contains criticism, commentary, bibliographies, and a wealth of other Beckett-related information and resources.

# References

Ackerley, C. J. and Gontarski, S. E. (2006), *The Faber Companion to Samuel Beckett*. London: Faber and Faber.

Anon (1953), 'Au Babylone et au Lancry – Deux coups heureux sur le damier du théâtre', Arts, 16 January. (Review).

Artaud, Antonin (1993), *The Theatre and its Double*. London: Calder.

Bair, Deirdre (1990), *Samuel Beckett: A Biography*. London: Vintage.

Beckett, Samuel (1952), *En attendant Godot*. Paris: Éditions de Minuit.

Beckett, Samuel (1965), *Waiting for Godot*. London: Faber and Faber.

Beckett, Samuel (1983), *Disjecta: Miscellaneous Writings and a Dramatic Fragment*, ed. Ruby Cohn. London: Calder.

Beckett, Samuel (1986), *The Complete Dramatic Works*. London: Faber and Faber.

Beckett, Samuel (1994), *Molloy*, *Malone Dies*, *The Unnamable*. London: Calder.

Billington, Michael (2006), 'Poignant elegy for the original odd couple', *Guardian*, 11 October. (Review).

Bradby, David (2001), *Plays in Production: 'Waiting for Godot'*. Cambridge: Cambridge University Press.

Brater, Enoch (2003), *The Essential Samuel Beckett: An Illustrated Biography*. London: Thames and Hudson.

Calder, John (ed.) (1967), *Beckett at Sixty: A Festschrift*. London: Calder and Boyars.

Cocteau, Jean (1948), *Antigone suivi de Les mariés de la Tour Eiffel.* Paris: Gallimard.

Coe, Richard (1964), (1968), *Samuel Beckett* (revised edn). New York: Grove Press.

Cohn, Ruby (1965), 'Philosophical fragments in the works of Samuel Beckett', in Martin Esslin (ed.), *Samuel Beckett: A Collection of Critical Essays.* New Jersey: Prentice-Hall, 169–77.

Cohn, Ruby (1973), *Back to Beckett.* Princeton: Princeton University Press.

Cohn, Ruby (1987), *From Desire to Godot.* Los Angeles: University of California Press.

Connor, Steven (1988), *Samuel Beckett: Repetition, Theory and Text.* Oxford: Blackwell.

Cronin, Anthony (1997), *Samuel Beckett: The Last Modernist.* London: Flamingo.

Driver, Tom (1961), 'Beckett by the Madeleine'. *Columbia University Forum*, 4 (3), 23–4.

Duckworth, Colin (1966), *Samuel Beckett: En attendant Godot.* London: Nelson.

Frère, Marcel (1953), *Combat*, 1 January. (Review).

Graver, Lawrence and Federman, Raymond (1979), *Samuel Beckett: The Critical Heritage.* London: Routledge.

Graver, Lawrence (2004), *Samuel Beckett: 'Waiting for Godot'* (2nd edn). Cambridge: Cambridge University Press.

Hall, Peter (1993), *Making an Exhibition of Myself.* London: Sinclair Stephenson.

Harmon, Maurice (ed.) (1998), *No Author Better Served: The Correspondence of Samuel Beckett & Alan Schneider.* London: Harvard University Press.

Hobson, Harold (1955), *Sunday Times*, 7 August. (Review).

Hobson, Harold (1956), 'Samuel Beckett – Dramatist of the Year'. *International Theatre Annual*, 1, 153–5.

Knapp, Bettina (1967), 'An interview with Roger Blin'. *Tulane Drama Review*, 7 (3) 111–25.

Knowlson, James (ed.) (1993), *The Theatrical Notebooks of Samuel Beckett. Volume 1: Waiting for Godot*. London: Faber and Faber.

Knowlson, James (1997), *Damned to Fame: The Life of Samuel Beckett*. London: Bloomsbury.

Knowlson, James and Knowlson, Elizabeth (2006), *Beckett Remembering, Remembering Beckett: Uncollected Interviews with Samuel Beckett and Memories of Those Who Knew Him*. London: Bloomsbury.

Lemarchand, Jacques (1953), *Figaro Littéraire*, 17 January. (Review).

Lyotard, Jean-François (1984), *The Postmodern Condition: A Report on Knowledge*. (trans. Geoff Bennington and Brian Massumi). Manchester: Manchester University Press.

Malpas, Simon (2005), *The Postmodern*. London & New York: Routledge.

McMillan, Dougald and Fehsenfeld, Martha (1988), *Beckett in the Theatre: The Author as Practical Playwright and Director. Volume 1: From 'Waiting for Godot' to 'Krapp's Last Tape'*. London: John Calder.

Mercier, Vivien (1956), *Irish Times*, 18 February. (Review).

Munk, Erika (1993), 'Notes from a trip to Sarajevo'. *Theater*, 24 (3), 15–30.

Oppenheim, Lois (ed.) (1994), *Directing Beckett*. Ann Arbor: University of Michigan Press.

Oppenheim, Lois (1995), 'Playing with Beckett's plays: On Sontag in Sarajevo and other directorial infidelities'. *Journal of Beckett Studies*, 4 (3), 25–46.

Oppenheim, Lois (ed.) (2004), *Palgrave Advances in Samuel Beckett Studies*. Houndmills, Basingstoke: Palgrave Macmillan.

Pavis, Patrice (1992), *Theatre at the Crossroads of Culture*. London: Routledge.

Rapp, U. (1985), 'Ambiguous Bonds'. *The Jerusalem Post*, 25 January. (Review).

Robbe-Grillet, Alain (1965), 'Samuel Beckett, or "Presence" in the Theatre', trans. Barbara Bray, in Martin Esslin (ed.), *Samuel Beckett: A Collection of Critical Essays*. Englewood Cliffs, NJ: Prentice-Hall, Inc.

Schumacher, Claude (1984), *Alfred Jarry and Guillaume Apollinaire*. Basingstoke: Macmillan.

Shuman, Milton (1955), 'Duet for two symbols'. *Evening Standard*, 4 August. (Review).

Sontag, Susan (1993), 'Godot Comes to Sarajevo'. *New York Review of Books*, 21 October, 52–9.

Sontag, Susan (2002), 'Waiting for Godot in Sarajevo'. *Where the Stress Falls: Essays.* London: Jonathan Cape and Random House, pp. 299–322. (This article is a slightly fuller version of the above *New York Review of Books* article.)

Taylor-Batty, Mark (2007), *Roger Blin: Collaborations and Methodologies*. Oxford: Peter Lang.

Trincal, Pierre (ed.) (1994), *Théâtre Aujourd'hui No. 3: L'Univers scénique de Samuel Beckett*. Paris: CNDP. (Audio CD).

Tynan, Kenneth (1955), *Observer*, 7 August. (Review).

Weitz, Soshana (1989), 'Mr Godot will not come today', in Hanna Scolnicov and Peter Holland (eds.), *The Play Out of Context: Transferring Plays from Culture to Culture*. Cambridge: Cambridge University Press, pp. 186–98.

Whitelaw, Billie (1995), *Billie Whitelaw . . . Who He?*, London: Hodder and Stoughton.

Woolf, Virgina (2003), *The Common Reader. Vol.I*. London: Vintage.

Worth, Katharine (1999), *Samuel Beckett's Theatre: Life Journeys*. Oxford: Clarendon Press.

# Index

Abbey Theatre (Dublin) 16
Abu-Varda, Yussef 74
Adamov, Arthur 52
Albery, Donald 58–9
*Andromaque* (Racine) 15–16
Anouilh, Jean 58
Apollinaire, Guillaume 31, 32
Aquinas, Thomas 24
Arafat, Yasser 75
Artaud, Antonin 14, 16, 31, 52, 98n
Arts Theatre (London), The 58
Asmus, Walter 39, 65, 67

Babylone, Théâtre, Le 52, 53, 59
Bair, Deirdre 53
Barbican, The 65
Bartók, Béla 63
Bateson, Timothy 60
*Be Big* (Laurel and Hardy) 27
Beckett Estate, The 73, 78
Beckett, Samuel
  as an academic 2, 15
  early writing 2–3
  education 2
  on form and content 31
  and the French Resistance 3–4
  on his work being
     understood 13–14, 81

interest in cinema 27
interest in theatre 15–16
and James Joyce 2–3
on Lucky 26, 43, 44
prose writing 5, 7–10, 14
on *Waiting for Godot* 20–1
writing for film and
     television 11, 17
writing in French 5–6, 18
writing for radio 11, 17
works
  *Act Without Words I*
     *and II* 11
  *All that Fall* 11
  *Cascando* 11
  'Dante . . . Bruno . . .
     Vico . . . Joyce' 2–3
  *Dream of Fair to Middling*
     *Women* 3
  *Eh Joe* 11
  *Eleuthéria* 5
  *Embers* 11
  *Endgame* 17, 66, 68, 81
  *Film* 11
  *Footfalls* 69, 73
  *Ghost Trio* 11
  *Happy Days* 17–18, 66, 68
  *Krapp's Last Tape* 66